More Advance Praise for *Trajectory*

"*Trajectory* maps out a range of effective approaches for achieving career goals. If you're stuck about what to do or where to go, this is a thought-provoking read."

—Adam Grant, Wharton professor and bestselling author of *Give and Take*

"As the HR leader of one of the world's most admired companies a prime focus of mine continues to be ensuring people develop meaningful and successful careers. The strategies in *Trajectory* will enable you to do just that. Consider this book essential reading if you are serious about owning and accelerating your career."

—David Rodriguez, Executive Vice President &
Chief Human Resources Officer, Marriott International

"Inspirational and achievable! Van Rooy combines science, history, and real-life examples in this powerful guide to fulfilling one's career destiny. Whether your goal is to find your own complete 'point of flow in career satisfaction' or achieve the highest levels in your field, *Trajectory* is a must-read to chart your path."

—Tom Waldron, Senior Vice President, People, Walmart

"*Trajectory* leaves you with tried and tested advice to advance your career. Whether you are just entering the job market or are already established at work, these timeless strategies will help you take control of your career to be more successful."

—Hon. Howard A. Schmidt, former Cyber Advisor
for President Bush and President Obama

"Continuous career development is something we all do. *Trajectory* brings together many of the most important aspects of a successful career into a compelling, easy-to-understand model for us all."

—Josh Bersin, Principal and Founder, Bersin by Deloitte

"In *Trajectory*, David Van Rooy describes the factors essential to success in business and life. It is a practical guide, complete with real-world examples that are both entertaining and instructive"

—Jim Weddle, Managing Partner, Edward Jones

"Personal authenticity coupled with introspection and action will take your trajectory to the highest heights. . . . I will be shocked if, after reading this book, you aren't motivated more than ever to go and do something purposeful about your career."

—Charles Baldwin, Executive Vice President & CAO, Cabela's

"*Trajectory* offers readers a crystal clear and actionable framework for anyone seeking to take charge of their career. Coupled with this framework is powerful advice that every professional should consider, regardless of where they are in their career journey. Without question, this book will be a primary tool in working with both my clients and students now, and well into future."

—Craig Williams, Ph.D., Vice President, Global Organizational
Effectiveness (retired); faculty, East Carolina University College of Business

"David Van Rooy's *Trajectory* is a pragmatic yet powerful synthesis of stories, concepts and advice on charting your career. Whether you are at the start, near the end or somewhere in the middle of your own trajectory, this book is a great read."

—Roger Cude, Enterprise Vice President,
Talent and Organization Development, Humana, Inc.

"David redefines the typical notions of career planning and success in *Trajectory*. This is a must-read guide if you want to learn effective and powerful strategies to move your career forward."

—Joanne Dahm, Co-President of Performance,
Talent and Reward, Aon Hewitt

"*Trajectory* is the career book you have been waiting for. David Van Rooy takes practical advice culled from real in-the-trenches experience, anchors it in research and history ranging from Seneca to Tony Hawk, and blends it with inspirational practical exercises to place you on the trajectory you desire. If your career matters to you, overlooking this book would be a mistake."

—Kaihan Krippendorff, author, *Outthink the Competition*,
and CEO, Outthinker

"Van Rooy's artful blending of research and storytelling makes *Trajectory* an indispensable resource for anyone who is serious about their career. Simply put, *Trajectory* is a groundbreaking book that will enable you to build and follow your roadmap for achieving career success."

—Daniel S. Whitman, Assistant Professor of Management,
Louisiana State University

DAVID L. VAN ROOY

TRAJECTORY

7 Career Strategies to Take You from
Where You Are to Where You Want to Be

AMACOM

AMERICAN MANAGEMENT ASSOCIATION

New York • Atlanta • Brussels • Chicago • Mexico City • San Francisco
Shanghai • Tokyo • Toronto • Washington, D.C.

This publication is designed to provide accurate and authoritative information in regard to the subject matter covered. It is sold with the understanding that the publisher is not engaged in rendering legal, accounting, or other professional service. If legal advice or other expert assistance is required, the services of a competent professional person should be sought.

© 2014 David L. Van Rooy
All rights reserved.
Printed in the United States of America.

LIBRARY OF CONGRESS CATALOGING-IN-PUBLICATION DATA
Van Rooy, David L.
  Trajectory : 7 career strategies to take you from where you are to where you want to be / David L. Van Rooy.
    pages cm
  Includes bibliographical references and index.
  ISBN-13: 978-0-8144-3390-4 (pbk.)
  ISBN-10: 0-8144-3390-1 (pbk.)
  1. Career development. 2. Success in business. I. Title.
  HF5381.V323 2014
  650.14--dc23
                        2013044170

About AMA
American Management Association (www.amanet.org) is a world leader in talent development, advancing the skills of individuals to drive business success. Our mission is to support the goals of individuals and organizations through a complete range of products and services, including classroom and virtual seminars, webcasts, webinars, podcasts, conferences, corporate and government solutions, business books, and research. AMA's approach to improving performance combines experiential learning—learning through doing—with opportunities for ongoing professional growth at every step of one's career journey.

Printing number

10 9 8 7 6 5 4 3 2

The author is donating all royalties from the sale of this book to the Institute for Veterans and Military Families (IVMF) in support of our veterans transitioning into the civilian workforce. IVMF's mission is to enhance competitiveness and advance the employment situation of veterans and their families by collecting, synthesizing, and sharing veteran-employment policy and practices; providing employment-related expertise, capacity, training, and education; and delivering technical assistance to stakeholders in the veterans' community. You can learn more about this organization at http://vets.syr.edu.

TO MY ANGELS

Ana Sofia

&

Ella Victoria

CONTENTS

INTRODUCTION

Without continual growth and progress, such words as
improvement, achievement, and success have no meaning.
—BENJAMIN FRANKLIN

In my career I have been extremely fortunate to work at some of the most recognizable and influential companies in the world, including Walmart, Marriott International, and Burger King. Collectively these three companies employ close to 3 million people in more than 100 countries around the globe. My current company, Walmart, has more than 2 million employees spread over 27 countries. Working at companies of this size and scope has given me an opportunity to build and experience programs and careers on a scale like no other. Over time, as I was growing my own career and contributing to these organizations, I was able to identify essential factors that lead to either career prosperity or disappointment and then develop career strategies based on those factors. In this book you will learn about those timeless strategies, which you can draw upon to ensure that you reach your goals and build the career you want.

My background and education draw from the emerging field of industrial-organizational (I/O) psychology, which is the area in which I obtained my Ph.D. At its core, the field is about both the psychology of the workplace and the psychology of the employee. Through understanding human psychology we can glean greater insights into human nature and help employees identify and harness their innate strengths and capabilities to maximize their performance and success in the workplace. This involves essential areas such as building better-functioning organizations and designing programs to hire and develop top employees.

What separates this book from so many others is the interplay of two key factors: my background in psychology coupled with my extensive global experience in massive organizations. Throughout this book I introduce classical and contemporary psychology studies to help explain the reasons behind why we do so much of what we do. However, I don't just talk about psychology with no basis in reality. And I don't just talk about experience with no basis in underlying mechanisms. What I do is blend the two together in order to bring the concepts to life and provide strategies that you can use to drive your career forward.

The first time I recall ever using the word *trajectory* to describe the process of progression was when I was telling my younger sister (who was thinking about going to graduate school at the time) about my own trajectory related to school. I explained that what really matters is trying your hardest and doing better and better at each stage of your life (as an aside, she did ultimately decide to go and now owns a successful chiropractic clinic). My grades started off low in grade school, got better in high school, and then even better in college. Thankfully I used that positive trajectory and carried it over to graduate school, where I received top grades to graduate with distinction.

Once I entered the workplace the concept of trajectory began to further take hold for me at a key point in my career. Like many employees, I frequently sought out more seasoned employees for advice and career guidance (and I still do this). The advice and wisdom imparted by so many people is something for which I have always been grateful, and I owe much of my success to this. One day my coworker Kate unexpectedly asked me if I would be willing to meet with her to provide career advice. It was such a simple request, and one that I had asked of others many times. This time, however, someone was asking it of me. Up to that point I had never really given much thought to being the one who would provide guidance to others on this topic. Yet because I knew how valuable the feedback I received had been, I wanted to pay forward the favor that had been bestowed on me so many times. From that moment I began to formally develop the concept of trajectory, which is about continually working toward and fulfilling your goals. In this book you will be introduced to seven strategies, referred to as lessons, that you can use as a guide to build and manage your own personal career trajectory. The strategies we will cover are not only timeless but also apply across all job levels and industries.

Based upon many conversations with successful leaders, as well as my own experiences, I started to look for common themes, something insightful I could say to Kate. When we met, we spoke about her career goals and ways that she could start off her career on the right track. This conversation was soon followed by similar conversations with other employees. I quickly realized that employees are most concerned with their current jobs, and some about the next job. Most employees want to discuss something very specific related to one of these. While these are both important, I realized that the focus was still primarily short-term, particularly for those who were at an early stage in their careers.

People struggle when talking about career goals further down the road, and they often have not considered how their current job will prepare them for the next one, and the next one, and so on. I knew that if I wanted to give valuable career advice that would truly benefit the employees seeking it from me I would have to address the long term, and coach people to direct their efforts to achieve those future goals. In addition to preparing for today and tomorrow, you must learn to prepare yourself for what comes after what's next. You can think of your growth around what is Now, Next, and Then in your career so that you can amass the right portfolio of experience to prepare you for each step. Phrases such as "career goals" and "career path" were familiar to most people but did little to resonate with them or help them plan. *Trajectory* will enable you to throw those generic ideas out the window and instead focus on strategies that are more intuitively concrete and, more important, that you can manage.

Another common thread I found in my conversations with employees was a conflict between a fear of failure and a desire for instant success. I began to notice that people often operate at two extremes. On one end, they have an inherent fear of failure, which can limit their risk taking. On the other end, they want to attain success as quickly as possible. These two extremes are not normally compatible. Yet in my conversations with my employees, I found ways to balance out this dichotomy. I will share those strategies and secrets with you in *Trajectory*.

I have not only sought out career advice and been asked for it, but I have synthesized those conversations into an easily accessible series of lessons that anyone can apply to his or her own career objectives. My goal in writing *Trajectory* is the same that I have when sitting down with an employee who is looking for guidance. I want to help people chart their personal and professional courses in an exciting, invigorating way that's so intuitive, people will wonder why they haven't thought of it already. *Trajectory* will give you the guidance and stability you have been looking for, both now and into the future.

THE CONCEPT OF TRAJECTORY

The journey of a thousand miles begins with one step.

—LAO TZU

Every person has a trajectory. Your trajectory is the path you create for yourself. This book shows you how to own yours. The general idea has been around for ages, but it is rarely understood or consciously managed effectively. And when it is, people often take a narrow view based on traditional models that worked in the past. That is why *Trajectory* is critically important to helping you find relevant ways to manage and grow your career. Every organization has a culture and must decide if that is something it wants to manage intentionally. The companies that choose to do so are more successful in the long run. Just as organizational culture must be managed, you must manage your career—your trajectory.

And it is up to you to determine how you manage it. This book will make it immensely easier for you to do just that.

Thomas Jefferson was someone who knew his trajectory. Although he is remembered primarily as a Founding Father and the third president of the United States, his accomplishments were many. Jefferson did not attain that esteemed position by accident. In an era without the many modern conveniences we take for granted, including electricity, phones, and the Internet, he was amazingly productive. He spoke five languages. He was an architect. He was a lawyer. He was a congressman. He framed the Declaration of Independence. He founded a major university, the University of Virginia. The list goes on.

After each of his successes it would have been easy for Jefferson to settle into complacency, but he chose to never stop learning and sought to continually drive his trajectory upward. He pushed for the betterment of himself and those around him, often at considerable risk. He put his life on the line by committing an act of treason against Great Britain when he signed the Declaration of Independence. He did this because it was the right thing to do for his fledgling country, and he knew that it would lead to greater things. You too must do the right thing, always. Do not always opt for the easy thing, as it may not be as beneficial to your long-term trajectory.

We cannot all enjoy the phenomenal historical significance of Jefferson, but each of us controls our own trajectory and success. Circumstance will influence your trajectory, but it is ultimately you who will choose it. From chaos and uncertainty comes opportunity. From opportunity comes growth. From growth comes success. As you will learn, you need to recognize and capitalize on those moments when growth can occur. Sometimes it is hard to do so amongst the daily turmoil, so you have to be deliberate and pull the positive lessons from every situation, including those that may seem negative at the time.

YOUR FOUNDATION

Creating a solid foundation is essential to your trajectory. You must establish strong core skills and continue to build upon those. Success builds more success. Even for our earliest ancestors, success developed over time. It is incremental progress that serves as the impetus for even faster progress. Consider the use of fire. Fire is something we all now take for granted, yet it is necessary for survival. From fire comes warmth and the ability to cook food. Only after this basic need was met could human civilization advance.

Keep in mind, however, that although fire is one of the earliest steps in a society's trajectory, it alone is not sufficient for true and sustained progress. You can build a bigger and bigger fire, but ultimately that will not equate to greater success in fire building. Similarly, bigger and bigger of the same thing in your career or organization is not necessarily always good. We will explore that idea in more detail in Lesson 5.

Consider too the human concept of numbers, another thing we take for granted. Anthropologists have identified the invention of a number system as a crucial step that begins to transform a primitive group of people into a civilized and educated society. A number system, even if it is as basic as using one's fingers to express the numbers, results in many desirable outcomes. Numbering leads to counting, and counting leads to bartering. Bartering leads to an economic system in which goods and services begin to obtain differential value. From this evolves a premium for certain skills and jobs. As these roles reap higher rewards, people can invest more in creating better services and products. As with fire, numbers provide a foundation to do even more.

It is not difficult to apply these basic principles to the world in which we live and work. These two simple examples demonstrate how success can evolve from simple beginnings. It is important to create and implement solid building blocks in your own life and career. It will be these foundational elements that will prepare you to manage your own personal trajectory and success in life. Just as organizations develop business strategies, you must create a career strategy for your trajectory. No company will be blindly successful over time without looking into the future and creating a plan. You will learn to do the same for yourself as you read this book. This is not to say you need to plot out your entire life. You simply need to plot it out far enough in advance to ensure that you keep moving your trajectory in the direction of your goals and aspirations.

WHERE TO BEGIN

It is never too early to start your trajectory. Remember the story about the red paper clip that was traded for a house? It started when Kyle MacDonald traded a simple red paper clip for a pen. He then traded the pen for something better, and continued to make trades until he ultimately was able to trade all the way up to a house. This so fascinated nine-year-old Brendan Haas that he decided to use the same idea—but in a different way. He realized he could leverage the general concept to do something very meaningful. He started by putting a toy soldier on Facebook to see what people would trade for it. He kept trading for bigger things and made several trades before ultimately swapping for an all-expenses-paid trip to Disney World. As planned, instead of keeping the trip he gave it away to a young girl who had lost her father in Afghanistan. Upon learning of his benevolent actions, Disney offered to give him another trip for himself. What did Brendan do? He gave it to a second child who also had lost a parent in war. Remember, Brendan was only nine years old. Brendan embarked on this journey with the goal of helping others. Even at this young age Brendan had a keen sense of his purpose and trajectory. Not only did he meet his initial goal, he was able to expand it and provide the same to another person.

A trajectory is rarely constant, and it does not need to be. A constant trajectory can actually be limiting if it is too flat. A more realistic—and common—trajectory is one that may include shallow rises, flat periods, and rapid ascensions. These can occur in any order, and you will likely have several periods of each over your career. Changes can occur within your current job or company, or could be driven by your desire to make a large transition, perhaps even into an entirely new line of work. Envision the stock market, but without it ever losing value for a sustained period of time. It may remain unchanged, lose short-term value, go up slightly, or it may spike dramatically upward. In your career you should expect and be prepared for similar dynamics along your trajectory. In this book you will learn more about how to prepare for and respond to these situations.

People often remark that you should think of work more as a marathon than as a sprint. It is not quite as simple as that. Your long-term trajectory and full career is the marathon; there will still be many sprints along the way. Give it your all at each step and focus on the moment, but do not lose sight of the long-term goal. Your short-term career strategy will inform and enable your long-term goals. Do not take a new job for short-term advantage; the new job must also serve as a setup to the next step in your career and trajectory. Many people look primarily at short-term gain, and in doing so compromise future opportunities. Jumping to a higher-paying job at every chance can result in nothing more than a hodgepodge of experiences that are not coherently integrated. Changing jobs often is not bad in and of itself, as long as you can string the jobs together to build the trajectory you want to achieve.

PERSISTENCE

Ben Saunders was devastated. He had failed in his dream to ski to the North Pole, something few others had accomplished. He was practically penniless. Gone were his visions of throngs of admirers meeting him upon his return at the airport and agents waiting with book and movie deals. He felt like a complete failure. But he had tried. He and his partner had made it two-thirds of the way to their goal. He began to consider what he could do differently and was determined that he would not give up on his dream. He was going to try again. He began planning and training for a second attempt. Not only did he decide to give it another try, but this time he was going to reach for something even harder—he was going to attempt the trek by himself.

During his solo attempt his progress was continually pushed backward. There were strong headwinds and whiteout storms. Temperatures dropped to fifty degrees below zero Fahrenheit. Large ice buildups required him to pull one sled, then go back and get the other. Sometimes this would require him to hike a total of three miles just to make it one mile forward. He persisted. While he slept at night the ice fields he had to cross floated him backward, as far as two and a half miles. He would spend hours in the morning reclaiming lost ground. Still he persisted. At various points the gaps in the ice were so wide that he had to don a dry suit and plunge into the water. He towed his sleds through the water like boats. He plowed on. After ten weeks he reached the North Pole—by himself! He was only the third person in history to accomplish this feat solo, and he did so ten years younger than anyone else before him.

After the first attempt to reach the North Pole, it would have been easy for Ben to say he gave it his best and not try again. But that was not his way. He had committed himself to a trajectory and pushed himself along it. He had persisted. Your journey may not be undertaken in such brutal physical conditions, but it will nonetheless be difficult in many other ways. We all encounter obstacles. As you will learn in Lesson 2, like Ben you also must push on. Headwinds may slow you down, but you must not let resistance stop you from reaching your goals and dreams.

A MATTER OF MINDSET

Cindy and Ron were both hired into similar roles on the same marketing team within two months of each other. Both were highly sought after by an outside recruiting firm and had outstanding credentials, including top university educations. Both left companies where they were highly regarded, and they chose to leave because of the tremendous opportunities provided by the new organization. Only one, however, was successful.

Shortly after they started their new jobs, their organization was acquired by another company. During this process great attention was given to creating a leaner organization and eliminating redundancy. They were both dismayed when they learned that their supervisor was part of the initial wave of layoffs. The new organization had acquired a significantly more diverse product portfolio through the acquisition, and both Cindy and Ron felt overwhelmed trying to understand the additional marketing complexities along with the management style of their new boss. Though both were disappointed in losing the supervisor they had come to work for and learn from, Cindy and Ron viewed their new situation differently from each other and chose diverging trajectories from that point forward. Cindy decided that this time of uncertainty could provide her with the visibility and jump-start she sought. Ron had a more cynical view and began to fear that he would be the next to be let go.

As the now combined organization progressed through the merger, Cindy began to learn more about the new strategy and how she could make a positive impact. She went out of her way to get to know many of the new leaders and ask for their perspective. During this time she received a great deal of advice, which she leveraged to further build out her own personal brand. She spent time with the individual product teams and learned about the pipeline and past marketing initiatives. She talked to customers to glean insights about the way they viewed the company and its products. As she continued through this process of discovery she became even more excited about her prospects for making a meaningful difference.

Ron also grabbed on to his work with a vengeance—but in the wrong way. As he was asked about his responsibilities, he was very resistant and protective of his area. At a time when the company was rapidly evolving, Ron was becoming more entrenched in his old ways. He felt that it would serve him well to show others how skilled he was in those areas. He began to emphasize his very strong technical skills, the same skills that had enabled him to differentiate himself from others early in his career. These ways had worked in the past, so he was sure they would work for him again in this time of uncertainty. Wrong. His technical skills were part of the reason he was hired, but it was his creative thinking that really stood out during the hiring process. And it was his creative thinking that he shelved out of fear of not showing tangible work. The new leadership team wanted people who were creative and could provide novel recommendations. He did not recognize or adapt to this need. By entrenching himself in his old ways out of a fear of change, he did not expand his thinking to find ways to identify and capitalize on new market opportunities. He had allowed himself to reach a point of stagnation, which is the topic of Lesson 5.

Ultimately Cindy developed and proposed a new marketing strategy to reshape how the combined organization would be positioned with consumers. She did this despite the fact that her formal job scope was actually limited to a single product line. Her recommendation was a resounding hit with her superiors and was eventually shared with the executive team and implemented. Moreover, her ability to search for opportunities and perform at a level above her job title was recognized, and it propelled her into an eventual promotion and long career with the company.

Not surprisingly the outcome was different for Ron. He languished for nearly two more years and struggled through some difficult feedback. He also began to build resentment toward Cindy as she continued to flourish and gain more responsibility. The organization was near the point of letting Ron go when he informed the company that he had found a new job. The role he accepted was at a smaller competitor and had less responsibility. In his exit interview he stated that he felt deceived after the acquisition, particularly after his boss was released. He further indicated that he did not think he received the resources and support he needed to succeed. This was obviously a bit perplexing since he and Cindy were in the same role on the same team. Ron could have chosen a better trajectory but opted to blame circumstance for his problems. Do not be like Ron. Do not use circumstances as a crutch or excuse. Be like Cindy. Flourish during times of uncertainty. Take the unexpected and use it to your advantage.

CREATING A TRAJECTORY

Each person's trajectory is different, because everyone's lives and motivations are different. Values, goals, and experiences all go into shaping your trajectory. Looking back on the first fifteen years of her career, Maria discusses many major milestones and changes. In Figure I-1 you can see how she has divided her career into three distinct chunks, each based on a different amount of time and milestones that were important to her. This is quite normal. Depending on where you are in your career and life, you may section out shorter or longer periods of time.

In Maria's trajectory you will notice that there are not just periods of rapid growth and change, but also extended periods of relative flatness. At every stage you should consider where you are, and whether you should modify or extend any part of your desired trajectory. When you do this you will be able to match your preparation and readiness to opportunity. There often are opportunities, but people aren't prepared. Or

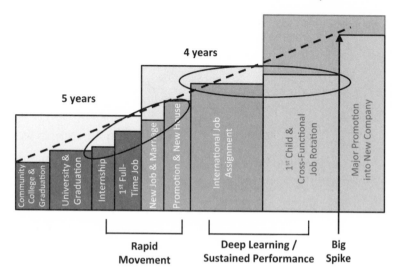

Figure I-1: Maria's Trajectory

someone is prepared and there is no opportunity. When you effectively manage your trajectory you will be able to match preparation with opportunity, something that many people fail to deliberately consider during their careers.

Through all of these periods and milestones you should pause along the way for introspection to ensure that you are still doing that which is important to you. Do not blindly continue to pursue a goal that has less meaning to you now than it once did. Maybe you once wanted to be a high school principal, but you truly love your present role as a seventh-grade teacher. That is great. Do not feel compelled to leave just because you previously thought that being a high school principal was your career aspiration. That's one of the wonderful things about your trajectory: it's yours. And it can change as your circumstances and aspirations evolve.

Maria had strong grades in high school, but for family reasons she opted to attend community college for the first two years after graduating. She knew all along, though, that she wanted to transfer into a large university afterward to get her bachelor's degree. With this goal in mind she received her associate's degree with a 3.9 GPA and was accepted into her college of choice. In addition, she received a large achievement-based scholarship award.

Maria chose a competitive major, and early on at the university decided that she needed to obtain an internship to maximize her chances of getting a good job after graduation. She began to establish relationships with professors, one of whom referred her for an internship. The internship did in fact provide her with the connections she needed; she was hired full-time at the company after the internship. This was followed by a series of quick promotions accompanied by major life events, including getting married and buying a house. Maria then made a major decision and decided to accept an international job assignment. This in retrospect was the starting point for a period of relative stability. Maria really enjoyed the assignment and stayed longer than she expected.

In conversations with her company about returning to the United States, Maria was offered a promotion or a chance to work in another department. Maria and her husband had been trying to start a family, and she did something that five years earlier she never would have imagined: she turned down

a promotion she wanted. She did so after coming to the real-
ization that she was at a point at which having a baby was
more important to her than her lofty career goals and progression. Looking back she says that this turned out to be one
of the best decisions she ever made. She had the child she
wanted but also learned an immense amount in the new job,
which resulted in her receiving an unexpected job offer from
another company at nearly double the pay. When she maps
her trajectory on paper she marvels at how the flattest part of
her trajectory is actually when she learned and grew the most.
She does not believe she would have been offered or prepared
for her current job had she not had that stable period. The
other jobs provided her with the skills and confidence to
know that she would succeed. We will discuss such stable
periods in more detail in Lesson 4 on plateaus.

It would be easy to compare the leveling off of Maria's
trajectory to the earlier, steeper trajectory, but that would be
a mistake. As you progress, you may spend more time at each
stage as the scope of your jobs continues to increase. As you
progress higher it will become increasingly difficult to move
up, and you will need to continue to develop your skills and
increase your knowledge even more to prepare yourself for the
next opportunity in your trajectory. In Maria's case, the flatter
lateral period involved gaining experiences that propelled her
even beyond where she expected to be at that point in her
career. Because of how well she managed it, her actual
trajectory became better than her planned trajectory. Each of
the steps in Maria's career may appear easy in isolation. The
real magic comes from consciously determining in advance

how to string these together such that each step better prepares you for the next. Like snowflakes, no two trajectories are ever the same, but each can be absolutely perfect in its own way.

A NOTE ABOUT JOB LOSS

At this point you might be wondering whether it's possible to prevent your trajectory from pointing downward at some point. Unexpected events occur. As we will discuss in Lesson 6, failure happens all the time. Sometimes the failure is small; sometimes it's big. Most obviously the latter happens when someone loses his or her job. The job loss may occur when companies merge, when organizations downsize and out-source, or when a major mistake or misjudgment is made. Surely if you lose your job your trajectory points downward, right? Not quite. The answer is completely dependent upon you and how you react to the situation. In general no one looks forward to losing a job, and being unemployed can create great stress. But it can also create great opportunity—opportunity that you might otherwise never be in a position to realize.

My friend Cathy was in a role in which she was responsi-ble for an organizational restructuring and served as the face of the company in dismissing hundreds of employees. At the end of the process, her boss told her she did a great job, and then told her that her position was also being eliminated. Through the process Cathy had witnessed how so many peo-ple reacted to this bad news. Now she had to determine how she would react.

For years she had talked about wanting to be a nurse but could never bring herself to give up such a well-paying job to go back to school. Upon being laid off she finally did just that. Her first reaction was one of anger at her boss. She felt that he and the company were ungrateful for all that she had done. She thought about suing them for wrongful termination. She seriously considered a job offer she received afterward from a competitor. But I think she took the best path possible—she pursued her dream. Of course, she did not plan on her trajectory including getting fired, but to this day she considers getting fired one of the best points of her career. If that had not happened, she never would have been able to establish her true trajectory.

Ken, who was a vice president and had been with his company for more than twenty years, also lost his job rather unexpectedly. He had many outside business connections, but most of them believed that because he had spent so much time with one company his skills were not transferable. This was actually not the case; he had developed a tremendous set of skills over the course of his career. During his time with the company he remained active in many outside groups and boards. He was the consummate learner. Immediately after being released he began to do pro bono work for several nonprofit organizations. He also reentered the job market. Ken says that the pro bono work energized him in a way he had not experienced in years. He was working on projects that were close to his heart. This enthusiasm carried over and resulted in his getting a new job as a senior executive in another firm. Similar to Cathy, Ken told me that he would never have found the new job if he had not been kick-started by getting fired. He had not even entertained the idea of looking for another job until that point.

Both Cathy and Ken—who chose positive but different ways to react—emerged from their unfortunate circumstances stronger and happier than before. In doing so they kept their trajectories from pointing downward. They used the experience as a point of learning and a springboard. The point of this book is not to argue that getting fired is good, nor is it about answering every question regarding what to do if you get fired. But if you do find yourself in that situation, you must realize that you can overcome it. You still control your trajectory. In fact, a juncture such as job loss is the most important time of all to own it.

Before we get into the seven lessons, let's start off with your first exercise, which you'll find on the next page.

EXERCISE

For this exercise you will look back over the previous five years of your life and then look forward for the same amount of time. First, on the Notes page write down all of the major events that occurred in your life and career during the past five years. What are the major milestones? Are there any points at which you lost ground? Why? What can you learn from that period? Next, look forward and map out the major milestones you expect to achieve over the upcoming five years. If you have not yet thought about this, now is a good time to start. What skills do you need to develop to reach your five-year goals? What relationships do you need to build? What obstacles do you need to remove? Now for the fun part: Combine your information to create a visual representation of your ten-year trajectory (five years back plus five years forward), similar to the one in Figure I-1.

NOTES

THE POWER OF FEEDBACK

Feedback is the breakfast of champions.

—KEN BLANCHARD

One of the easiest ways you can help yourself create and maintain a solid trajectory is to proactively seek out feedback. When I am talking about feedback, I mean hard feedback. Real feedback. Not softballs and platitudes to make you feel good about yourself. During the course of your career you should continually seek out those individuals who don't pull punches. It is easy—and common—for people to request feedback when they know it is going to be positive. It is much harder to request feedback when you think it may be critical of you. It is this feedback that is most valuable and that allows you to learn about your weaknesses. This information will enable you to chart a course to improve upon those areas. And you must begin to view feedback as a routine practice. Starting now.

Incidentally, the simple act of asking for feedback can propel you forward, assuming you respond favorably to it. Doing so shows that you are interested in continual learning, bettering yourself, and improving your performance in order to further your success as well as the company's. Leaders like success and success stories. Through receiving feedback and making positive changes you become a success story yourself. I have heard conversations many times about employees who are quite similar, but one is held in higher regard because of that person's tendency to seek out feedback.

In this lesson you will learn about ways to ask for and receive feedback. While on the surface it seems easy to ask for feedback, it can be very daunting and even intimidating. This is particularly true when you are not sure what you are going to hear, or are afraid that asking might be perceived as a sign of weakness or insecurity. Obtaining really useful feedback, called *deep feedback*, starts by knowing how to properly ask for it. All too often people never receive deep feedback due to missteps out of the gate when requesting it. On the receiving end, you must know how to avoid common mistakes that can easily occur based on your reaction to deep feedback. Deep feedback is about the truth, and without it you will have much more difficulty identifying your weaknesses and improving in those areas. If you realize that this hard feedback gets to the truth you will then be able to work on your weaknesses and even turn those areas into strengths.

NEGLECTING TO ASK

One of the most fateful mistakes people make is to assume they have all the answers. You must realize that the era in which asking for help was considered a sign of weakness is long gone. The best leaders actively seek out help, thereby gaining critical insight to aid in growing their skills and planning their trajectory. People often misconstrue what feedback is really about. It is not about people saying "great job," and it is not just about seeking out accolades from others. In contrast to deep feedback, this is *surface feedback*. While surface feedback is important to receive when you do something well, it does little to provide you with constructive guidance for improvement. What we are going to talk about in this lesson includes how to ask the difficult questions to get at the information that may be critical in nature and hardest for you to hear, but most relevant to your success. To be able to seek out valuable feedback you must build the necessary internal fortitude to accept what you might uncover. Most important, you must empower people to feel comfortable providing you with the unvarnished truth.

My friend Doug worked in a Fortune 100 company and had quickly built a reputation as someone who delivered results during his two years with the organization. He also built another reputation, a reputation unknown to him: arrogance. Unfortunately, he had received only surface feedback on his results in the past. "Doug, great job on the Mercury Project." "Doug, I can't believe you pulled off that new launch in six months. Amazing!" Understandably,

Doug thought he was doing very well. But trouble was lurking under the surface. The company where he worked had a policy that required each manager to participate in a 360-degree review every few years. With a 360 review, input is gathered from a broad range of people, including peers, supervisors, subordinates, and customers. Doug expected to get very encouraging feedback and was excitedly waiting for the positive comments and the promotion that was sure to follow. Instead he was mortified when he received the results.

Rather than a list of accolades, Doug was staring at multiple low ratings and qualitative feedback that was difficult for him to digest. He could not believe that the results were actually his. He began to think back over the past two years and could not pinpoint specific incidents that would have led to this feedback. He was debriefed on the results by a professional coach, who recommended that he meet individually with each person who had provided input into the 360 review. Furthermore, he instructed Doug to give colleagues and coworkers permission to give him honest feedback during their face-to-face meetings. Giving people permission to be transparent is incredibly important. Other than your direct boss, few people have a vested interest in being candid with you. In fact, many people are reluctant to give feedback outside of their area, as there is often not much upside to doing so. Doug followed his coach's advice, and what he encountered would change him for the rest of his career.

It all started with his first meeting with Antonio, who was a director in another department. Antonio had interacted with Doug numerous times on cross-functional projects, and they had a good working relationship. During the meeting Antonio provided input that really opened Doug's eyes. The conversation went as follows:

DOUG: Antonio, thank you for taking the time to meet, and for participating in my 360 review. I received positive feedback in a number of areas, including executing projects on schedule. However, there was also consistent feedback from the 360 that my style was perceived as condescending and even arrogant by some people. I would like to ask for your unvarnished feedback directly. Your opinion means a great deal to me, and I know I can improve based upon it.

ANTONIO: Well, Doug, that's a tough question. You have done a pretty good job completing the projects that you have been assigned. But I've also been troubled by the way you came across to my team. Instead of seeking out their opinions, you always would directly jump to providing yours. You might have been right, but my team thought that you ignored them and were more interested in showing off how much you know. They really felt that you did not care to take the time to listen to their ideas.

DOUG: Wow, I never realized they felt that way. Why haven't you told me this before?

ANTONIO: Because you never asked. My biggest concern
was the success of the projects, and I did not want to
interfere with the feedback that I am sure your boss
was already giving you on this.

DOUG: But I never heard this from my boss . . .

Doug had made a cardinal mistake. He believed he was
doing well across the board, and assumed that he would be
given feedback even if he didn't ask for it. In this case, however, his boss did not witness what others on the project
teams were experiencing. Had Doug asked for feedback earlier he could have self-corrected before the negative reputation spread. To Doug's immense credit, he took it a step
beyond what his coach recommended. He began to understand how his behavior could have been interpreted that way,
and vowed to change it. He met with the people he had impacted and had open conversations about what it would be
like to work with him moving forward. The people he spoke
with appreciated his candor, and luckily Doug was able to
regain his footing. Several years later Doug remarked that the
360 felt like a punch to the stomach, but it was an awakening
moment. Since then as a matter of practice he routinely asks
for feedback at various points in all projects. His receptive-
ness to feedback and change has even been held up as an example in various meetings. He laughs now and says, "The
good thing is that I am now used as an example. The bad
thing is that I let myself get to that point."

OVERCOMING YOUR OWN RESISTANCE

Many people are adamant that they already know what they do well and what they don't do well. Nothing could be further from the truth. We can certainly make these judgments in broad and sometimes irrelevant areas, but we do not do so well when evaluating specific skills and competencies. For instance, a manager may know that he is not a good guitar player. However, in considering his career, he may erroneously believe that people think he is pleasurable to work for. Quite simply, people are not good judges of their own skills, particularly ones in which they are not strong. Ask ten people if they think they are above-average drivers. Seven or more people are likely to say yes. Ask ten other people if they are above-average parents. Eight or more will likely say yes. Yet it is obviously not possible for everyone to be above average. Incidentally, people with higher intelligence have been found to have even less awareness of their weaknesses than do others. Remember this the next time you think you are attuned to your strengths and weaknesses and therefore do not feel a need to seek feedback.

To further illustrate how wide the gap is between our own and others' perceptions, consider performance evaluations. Research has consistently revealed that people are notoriously bad at rating their own performance; the correlation between self-ratings and manager ratings across many studies has been shown to be moderate at best. Still, organizations continue this practice, largely because it makes people feel good. What really happens is that self-ratings distract from receiving the important feedback that is so essential for your development and growth. In your conversations with your boss, focus less on the ratings you receive, and push to get to the deep feedback that you need. When you let go of numbers and ratings you open yourself up to receiving substantive feedback that you can actually use.

Other times something seems so basic that you may not even consider the need for feedback. This can lead to negative consequences. The Coors Brewing Company had a now infamous example of this. Desiring to extend the ad campaign for its "Turn it loose" slogan, Coors had the phrase translated for the market in Spain. Unfortunately, the subsequent translation was interpreted as "Drink Coors, suffer from diarrhea." Coors obviously knew that the campaign was important, as evidenced by the budget to produce and deliver it. Yet feedback was not requested from those who knew this area the best: bilingual speakers who were native to the target country. An embarrassment could have been avoided in a matter of minutes if this type of feedback had been sought. This example is a bit humorous, but the principle applies everywhere. Be careful when you are so close to something that you cannot see the forest for the trees. Do not assume you know.

It is also easy to dismiss feedback, not just because you disagree with it, but because other things seem more important at the time. When this happens, the area of concern will usually resurface later, when it will be even more of a problem. Howard Schultz, the chairman and CEO of Starbucks, describes such a situation. For years the emphasis at Starbucks had been on the growth of the chain. Starbucks had been growing so quickly that feedback that could impede expansion was brushed under the rug. Schultz relates the story of problems that reemerged in the Starbucks distribution network when he returned as CEO after resigning eight years earlier. He had heard the feedback and complaints about the company's supply chain organization (SCO) before, but he simply instructed people to get products to the stores; he did not mandate the necessary investment to address the underlying issue. He now uses this oversight as an example of ignoring something that should have been an obvious need requiring action. SCO was not an area in which he had a deep interest, and therefore he did not devote the necessary attention to building it out properly. As a result, he came back to find the supply chain organization in even greater disarray. It was now impacting the ability to get products to the Starbucks locations. Ultimately he was able to resolve the problem, but the level of effort to do so was way beyond what it would have been had he acted earlier. Lesson: It is easier to step out of a pothole than a pit.

This same tendency to dismiss feedback can further manifest itself during times of success. Do not let success preclude you from seeking feedback. If you are not careful, success itself can become the biggest barrier to recognizing and dealing with what is in front of you. Remember to focus on not just the previously unknown feedback you uncover from others, but also on what you already know and have avoided or ignored. In particular, pay attention to feedback relating to those shortcomings that you have been able to mask because of success in other areas.

If you do not actively seek and consider feedback you will succumb to what is known as *bounded awareness*. As described in their *Harvard Business Review* article, Max Bazerman and Dolly Chugh illustrate how people fail in their awareness to see what is right in front of them. People often focus only on obvious areas, and therefore their ability to improve suffers because they are not using all of the information available to them. We are inclined to focus on very specific and salient information, while missing other information that is readily available. To illustrate the point, Bazerman and Chugh relate this failing to a famous experiment in which people watched a video and were asked to count how many times a basketball was passed. Almost everyone was so focused on watching and counting the basketball passes that they failed to notice that a person in a gorilla costume walked right through the middle of the court! The participants were successful in counting the number of basketball passes but had missed so much else. At work and in life you must not focus so closely on one thing that you don't even notice the gorilla in the middle.

DEPERSONALIZATION

Seeking feedback sounds quite easy. It is just a matter of asking someone for it, right? Wrong. It is relatively easy to ask for, but then the moment arrives when you receive the unvarnished truth. It is at this moment that you will test yourself. Your reaction is critical. Do not rationalize the feedback or explain it away. Do not blame others. Do not get angry. If you react in any of those ways, you are less apt to receive accurate feedback from that person again. No, you need to take in the feedback. Process it. Remember, this person's opinion does matter or you would not have asked for it in the first place. If you are not sure about what you have heard, ask clarifying questions. Request a specific example. If the feedback is hard to hear, thank the person and then go digest it. Do not react defensively. Taking this approach will allow you to introspectively process the feedback and then come back another day to continue the discussion.

The way that you choose to accept feedback can be broken down into *constructive* reactions and *destructive* reactions. People often talk about receiving constructive feedback, but it can only be effective if you also react constructively to it. All too often people do the opposite and let feedback that is given with positive intentions spiral into a negative situation. There is nothing worse that can happen with feedback than allowing a constructive moment to turn into a destructive event. If you make that mistake, what was intended to be a helpful encounter can quickly turn into a situation that leads to resentment.

A prior employee of mine, Jeff, who was an outstanding performer, found a way to avoid reacting destructively to feedback. When presented with difficult feedback he would listen very attentively, perhaps ask a few clarifying questions, and then simply say, "Thank you for the feedback." Like clockwork, he would return a few days later and ask if we could talk about it some more. Jeff just wanted time to process before reacting. This was important to him because he did not want to risk coming across as defensive or resistant to the feedback. Jeff would take the time to think about what he'd heard and then come back with additional questions and a plan that he had started to create to address the opportunity. In doing so Jeff was able to react to feedback in a constructive manner.

What Jeff was doing was utilizing an approach to depersonalize the feedback. When you get feedback you must not personalize the conversation. Remember, the purpose of feedback is not for you to win a popularity contest; it is for you to improve your performance. To enable this you must not take the feedback personally. You can be transparent when seeking clarity, but you should avoid adopting a "you-versus-them" mentality.

Consider Jeremy, who took a different approach that turned into destructive feedback. His intent was to improve on some specific developmental opportunities that his supervisor reviewed with him during his performance evaluation. During the evaluation his supervisor suggested that he speak with his peer Alana, with whom he had worked on many projects. As Alana began to provide him with suggestions and specific examples, Jeremy interrupted and said, "I don't know why you have to always bring that up. When are you going to let go of the fact that we missed the deadline on the Atlas Initiative?" The conversation quickly went downhill from there. Instead of objectively working through how the same mistakes could be avoided in the future, Jeremy had personalized his reaction and put Alana in a difficult position. When Alana relayed this story to me, I was not surprised to hear that she did not want to go out of her way to provide Jeremy with feedback in the future. Not only did Jeremy miss an important opportunity to improve, but he also cut off an avenue of future feedback and potentially harmed a working relationship.

An example that hit even closer to home occurred when I provided a colleague with feedback to help her improve the way in which she communicated messages to executives. What was Sheila's response? "I have never heard that from anyone else, so I don't see any need for me to change my style." Her reaction certainly left me not wanting to go out of my way to help her in the future. This situation did at least end well. Upon giving it some thought, she asked a few others about the feedback and learned that the perspective was actually pervasive. However, the bad taste I had from the experience could have been avoided entirely had Sheila not personalized the feedback and acted defensively. In addition, like Doug, Sheila had erred in thinking that just because she had not heard the feedback before that everything must be going well. It should be clear by now that you must be careful not to make this mistaken assumption.

Another lesson within Sheila's response is to pay attention to perception. Even if you adamantly disagree, someone else's perception is still important. Stories can build and spread quickly, and this is often what happens if you do not address that perception. You need to ask those clarifying questions, seek specific examples, and then work to change the perception that you think is incorrect.

FEEDBACK FROM MENTORS

One of the best ways for you to gather feedback is through mentoring. Mentors can provide you with an accelerated path to learn from others. If there are people in your desired career job, or in a job along the path to it, seek them out. Build a relationship with and gain insights from them. They likely did not get there by chance and undoubtedly could talk at length about what they learned along their trajectory. This is invaluable. Given the choice to attain certifications, attend training, or participate in any of the other du jour organizational activities available, always take a knowledgeable and attentive mentor first. Among all the advantages of doing so, perhaps the best is that mentors can provide one of the most neutral outlooks on your performance. This makes it even easier for you to ensure that you can maintain a depersonalized perspective when receiving feedback.

Mentoring is not just for junior-level employees. Even mentors have mentors. Top-level executives—including CEOs—have mentors. Far from being above the need for a mentor, successful leaders have a great appreciation for the value a mentor provides. Helpful feedback can be considered a gift, in turn making a mentor a gift. And if you are at a point at which it is possible, reciprocate. Return the gift by also serving as a mentor. Mentoring is valuable not only for the mentee, but also for the mentor. A great deal can be learned through giving constructive feedback along with monitoring and responding appropriately to the recipient's reaction.

A common mistaken impression with mentoring is that it is about a one-way relationship with someone at a higher level in the organization. The truth is that you can learn from so many other "mentors." For example, Alex was a manager in a mid-size organization and had a mentor with whom he had been working. His mentor was a senior leader in the same job function and was a great resource for his development. However, Alex had mapped out his trajectory and knew that two or three years down the road he wanted to move into a different function. What he did may surprise some but is actually a very good approach for expanding professional development. He found a mentor who was at a lower level than he was, but importantly was in the function he wanted to learn. This approach to mentoring provided him with a way to gain critical knowledge and prepared him to eventually land a job in that department.

Another very effective approach is to gather feedback from participating in or leading a *mentor circle*. In a mentor circle an individual leads a mentoring event with multiple people at the same time. This method enables a unique group dynamic and presents a great opportunity for discussing business challenges. In doing so, many people get a chance to learn simultaneously from a leader rather than only interacting one-on-one. In addition, this is a great chance for a leader to learn from others by seeking multiple viewpoints and suggestions for various situations and business scenarios.

It is important that you consider the purpose of mentors and other people in guiding your career. Your goal should not be to reach success through others. Other people can help you, but don't look to them to create your success. You should instead invest more time in creating your own. The purpose of having a mentor is to acquire valuable insights and obtain professional growth, not nepotistic professional gain. The difference sounds subtle, but it is not. You should not seek out a mentor solely in hopes that the person can help you find another job or get you promoted. If that happens, great, but it should be a by-product. Instead, your mentors should serve to impart their wisdom and learning to you. It is ultimately this gift that matters. Organizations change and leaders come and go. If you do not learn from your mentor and are only using the person for professional gain, you also risk having wasted considerable time should that individual leave the organization.

Once you have a mentor, your primary purpose needs to be to learn. Doing so will require you to develop the skill of being a good listener. Resist the urge to be an expert or have an opinion on everything, and you will be able to learn tremendously from others. There is an old saying attributed to Epictetus that states, "You have two ears and one mouth—use them in that proportion." Remember this as you have conversations with mentors. It is not always as important to show what you know as it is to show that you can listen and learn.

CAPITALIZING ON FEEDBACK

Many organizations are limited in their growth strategies only by the available talent of their employees. They have the financial capital to grow, but not the talent. It is your job to take advantage of this fact. In-N-Out Burger, which we will discuss in more detail in Lesson 2, made a conscious decision to never build new restaurants faster than it was able to develop quality restaurant managers. Through proactively seeking feedback you can achieve a competitive advantage and position yourself ahead of those who are not doing the same. All things being equal, one of the best things you can do is gain an edge through feedback. If you do this and another employee does not, you have just moved a step ahead. In addition to getting the feedback needed to grow, you have done something else. You have positioned yourself in the eyes of others as someone who cares about his career and the company. You have sought their opinion in an effort to perform better. You have further built out relationships and created more advocacy from those who provided feedback. With all of the benefits of feedback, it is a wonder that seeking it is not more common. Seek it proactively and prepare to reap the rewards it will give you.

The best time to seek feedback is often when you least expect to need it. Perhaps you took something for granted that you should not have. Confidence is an important and admirable trait, but do not let it get in the way of seeking advice. Jan learned this the hard way. She had been in her role for nearly a year and a half, and truly enjoyed what she was doing. Her goal was not to move to another department, but to take on more responsibility through a promotion in her current role. The organization had a process for candidates to apply for a within-role promotion, and she jumped at the opportunity. Her performance to that point had been stellar, and she received nothing but rave reviews from the various people with whom she had worked. But Jan did not get the expected promotion.

What happened? Jan had erroneously concluded that the promotional process was just a formality and that she would be given the promotion based on her exceptional performance, which everyone had recognized. Unfortunately Jan had misjudged, and did not put herself in a position to capitalize on proactive feedback. The individuals involved in the process also had expected her to do well, and were shocked as she stumbled through it. When her supervisor delivered the bad news, Jan was even more surprised because she thought she had done quite well through the process.

The lesson that Jan ultimately took away was that unsubstantiated assumptions can be reckless. In a central part of the promotional process Jan had mistakenly assumed that the focus was on something different from what it actually was. If Jan had paused for a moment to ask a simple clarifying question she likely would have breezed through the process. She could have cleared up any confusion and obtained a better outcome had she just asked something as simple as this: "In order to prepare for the promotional process I have been preparing in three areas. Is my focus in each of these areas on track, and are there other areas I should be considering?"

Jan learned from this and performed spectacularly the next time the opportunity for promotion was available. She also expressed disappointment in herself for not taking the time to ask that simple question up front the first time. In a recent conversation Jan remarked, "I couldn't believe that they would not promote me, because my performance track record was so strong, but I understand I had left them with no choice. The process reminded me that I should not take outcomes for granted, and I now carry this with me all the time to ensure that I am continually at my best."

DON'T JUST LOOK UP

It is also important that you resist the tendency to ask only people in higher positions for feedback. Some of the best and most insightful feedback will come from peers, colleagues, and even subordinates. These are the people who get to see and interact with you the most, and you must not discount the importance of the feedback you can glean from them. Though superiors have more direct decision-making control for your next career move, other groups have considerable indirect control. How? Through giving you advance notice of those areas you need to develop. They can see these things before your leaders notice them, thereby giving you a wonderful opportunity to adjust proactively. Similarly, as Alex demonstrated, another effective approach is to seek feedback from people in different departments. Those employees often have helpful perspectives based on their focus on other parts of the business.

The same holds true when you are considering possible mentors. You must pick a mentor who has experiences aligned with your aspirations. Do not simply jump to get a mentor who has the highest position. It is certainly nice to get access to someone with a big title, but you must also consider the quality of the feedback you will receive relative to your desired trajectory. Look for individuals who have taken a path similar to the one you are pursuing. Or look for mentors in related business functions who can provide unique insights that will enable you to perform even more effectively in your role. This is a quick way to find differentiators that allow you to separate yourself from others.

You must also consider that your specific job is just one part of a much larger feedback machine that you must enable. When you look all around you will be able to find feedback from many different sources. As you will learn in Lesson 5, keeping up with rapid advancements is essential to maintaining your trajectory. If you look at Figure 1-1 you will notice that your job is the center of your work environment, but there are multiple other sources you must draw from. If you put all of the other circles in this knowledge circle together you will notice that collectively this covers a much larger area than just your job. You cannot neglect to get feedback from people in these other areas. By tapping into each of them you will find ways to continually adapt and learn the necessary new skills fast enough to stay ahead and on your trajectory.

ENVIRONMENTAL-BASED FEEDBACK

Another excellent way to gain feedback is through observation, both behavioral and outcome-based. A great example of this

Figure 1-1: Feedback Knowledge Circle

is seen in Sam Walton, the founder of Walmart, who was renowned for learning from others. In fact, he even stated that he had no shame in learning from his competition and building and modeling stores after the best of what he found when visiting them. What he realized is that it is not always necessary to reinvent the wheel. In fact, I would argue that in most of your pursuits this will not be prudent. Sam Walton capitalized on this when he emulated and improved upon his competition in areas in which they were doing a great job. What he recognized is that there are few substitutes for on-the-ground experience.

There is a breakout that many companies and scholars use when discussing the best way for people to learn, expressed in percentages: 70-20-10. The percentages signify the amount of time that should be spent learning in different formats. Seventy percent should be experience-based. That is, get right into the actual environment and get real-time feedback from doing. Twenty percent should be exposure-based, which means watching and learning from others doing. The final 10 percent is educational, which is learning through formal classes and training. As this breakout shows, there is no substitute for environmental-based learning and feedback. It is so important that you should spend nearly three-quarters of your time learning this way if possible.

Psychologists refer to this in various applications as *psychological fidelity*. With high fidelity something closely matches the actual environment in which it would occur. When Sam Walton visited stores he was using high-fidelity learning. A bank teller taking a high-fidelity training simulation might actually process banking transactions that mimic real-life customer interactions that could be expected on the job. Flight simulators for pilots must have extremely high fidelity to ensure that pilots are trained under the most realistic situations possible for flight of an actual aircraft. By identifying environmental-based opportunities for experience you can create a much higher fidelity, and thereby increase the knowledge and skill transfer back to your job.

Through these environmental experiences you get real-time feedback on how to do things better.

UNCONSCIOUS FEEDBACK

A great deal of attention has been given to how you can actively (i.e., consciously) learn from others through feedback and other mechanisms. Not nearly enough attention is given to the processes behind *unconscious feedback*. What many people don't realize is that feedback is nothing more than a learning mechanism, albeit a critical one. You get feedback all the time. It is all around you. With unconscious feedback you are learning even if you may not directly realize it at the time. A prime example of this is found in children as they begin to acquire language and the ability to speak. They don't realize they are learning; they unconsciously begin to pick up words as they hear others around them speak.

A classic psychological study by Dr. Albert Bandura shows us how easily we learn from observing others and how quickly something can become ingrained—even unconsciously—as we do so. Bandura sought to better understand how people learn and are influenced by others, and he designed a creative study to test his hypothesis. At the core of his experiment was a five-foot-tall "bobo doll" (which, some of you may remember, usually is an inflated figure that when pushed, kicked, punched, etc., will bounce right back up). Children were individually placed in a room with an adult who, as part of the experiment, would simulate behavior to see how the children would react later. In some cases the adult would behave aggressively, and in others nonaggressively toward the doll. Each child was then taken into another room that had toys that were considered both aggressive (bobo doll, a mallet and peg board, dart guns, etc.) and nonaggressive (tea set, crayons, stuffed animals, etc.) in nature.

What Bandura found was that being in and observing others in the environment had a powerful effect in determining subsequent behavior. Children who watched adults behaving aggressively later did the same when given the chance to play with other toys, including the bobo doll. Children who observed adults who did not behave aggressively instead reacted more mildly and playfully with their toys.

Unconscious feedback and its influence on you is immensely important when you consider that you likely spend more time with your coworkers than with your family and friends. To see how easily and quickly unconscious feedback can set in, try this simple test at work. Next time you are with a small group of people, look at your hand and comment that either your index finger or ring finger is longer (e.g., say "That's odd, I never noticed that my index finger was longer than my ring finger."). As soon as you hold up your hand to do this, others are then likely to look at their own hands. Though there is no relevance or scientific significance to the length of these fingers, people cannot help but look at their own for comparison purposes.

Unconscious feedback is gained through watching the mannerisms and body language of others. This ability to monitor your environment can give you real-time insight into what is resonating with people and what is not. Not only can you learn unconsciously yourself, you also can learn from the unconscious behaviors of others. For instance, an audience or attendees in a meeting may unconsciously give cues of being either engaged or bored during a presentation. The adept speaker picks up on this quickly and will adjust accordingly. The process of doing this could range from something subtle, like picking up on a look of confusion, to something more obvious, such as people holding sidebar conversations while you are speaking.

CONCLUSION

As you saw in the feedback knowledge circle (Figure 1-1), feedback is all around you. Your job is to find it, both through asking directly and observing it. Seeking the right type of feedback will enable you to solidify your strongest areas and embark on a journey to improve those areas that others deem to be weaknesses. With so many responsibilities at any given time it can be all too easy to forget to take the time to ask for feedback. If you neglect to ask, you increase the risk of continuing on a path that you will then need to backtrack. Think of feedback as a compass—something that when used frequently and correctly will keep you on your trajectory.

It is important, however, that you do not confuse feedback with advice. As discussed, feedback is based on another person's perception of you and is therefore a reality you need to consider. Advice, however, is input for you to consider in a decision-making process. On the one hand, let's say you ask for input on your performance and learn that others feel that you are not a team player. This is feedback. Whether you agree or not, this is their belief, and it may have an adverse effect on your interactions if you do not attempt to address it. On the other hand, imagine you are seeking opinions on a new product strategy you are developing. People may view the product differently from the way you do and provide you with alternatives to consider. Their input in that case is advice, and ultimately you will need to decide whether you want to accept it and refine or change your strategy.

Both feedback and advice are essential. The key difference is in short-term and long-term implications based upon how you receive each. If you do not address the feedback, you will be perceived as resistant to change and unwilling to grow. If you do not follow advice, your decision will be acceptable as long as you explain your reasons for going down an alternate path.

Let's move on to your next exercise before turning to Lesson 2.

EXERCISE

Pick a person with whom you have had a difficult relationship at work, and invite the person for coffee. Tell the individual in advance that you would like to seek input on what is working well and what can be improved. After you have processed the feedback, review it with your boss. Get your boss's perspective on it, and discuss what you will do to improve in this area. Then circle back with the person who provided feedback and review the changes that you will be making. Write down the commitments you made to the person on the Notes page. Regularly review these commitments to ensure that you are following through on the changes.

NOTES

PERSISTENCE AS A DIFFERENTIATOR

Nothing in the world can take the place of persistence.
Talent will not; nothing is more common than
unsuccessful men with talent.
—CALVIN COOLIDGE

Imagine that you were absolutely certain that you knew what you wanted and you were told up front that you could achieve it. There was nothing that you wanted more, and you would even risk your life to achieve it. But there is a catch: You would need to wait more than fifty years before you could fulfill your goal. Would you wait? Or would you seek out a different goal? Think about this for a moment.

Now imagine that not only would you have to wait five decades in order to achieve your goal, but twenty-seven of those years would be spent in the confines of a small prison cell. Maybe this is a goal that might not be worth the effort, and it would be good to focus on something else. Your friends would certainly understand if you moved on to a different pursuit. Nelson Mandela would have disagreed. Beginning in his teens, Mandela fought for the end of apartheid and the freedom of all South Africans. It was this struggle that led to a quest that lasted fifty-plus years, including the twenty-seven that he was forced to spend in prison.

During this time Mandela never lost sight of his goal and larger purpose, and throughout his imprisonment he persisted. In fact, in many ways his influence grew even stronger while he was in confinement. Upon his release in 1990 he immediately gave a speech to reinforce his beliefs in the importance of a free and nonsegregated country. Just four short years later the first multiracial election was held in South Africa and Mandela was elected as the first-ever black president of the country. In doing so he showed the world what true persistence is about and was able to progress a step further in his mission and trajectory.

As Nelson Mandela so poignantly exemplified, success is about more than just ability and luck. Of course, it didn't hurt that Mandela had both. He did have great ability, especially with instantly captivating a crowd and getting people to believe in his vision. And he was lucky that he wasn't sentenced to death and executed like some of his comrades. But those factors alone would not have enabled him to become a major historical influence recognized around the world. Thus, although ability and luck are important, persistence—a close cousin to motivation—is essential to maintaining the trajectory you desire.

It is persistence that truly differentiates those who are successful from those who are not. Leaders with this key attribute continually look into the future and set goals for themselves, regardless of any prior failures or setbacks. In fact, those with the greatest persistence use failure as a motivating factor to try again and do even more. Without persistence it is significantly more difficult to remain successful over time, which will limit your trajectory and potential for continual success.

THE PSYCHOLOGY OF PERSISTENCE

In the psychological literature there is a compelling body of research that has explored the factors that underlie successful performance. On the most simplistic level this research can be explained via a straightforward equation: *Ability* × *Persistence* = *Performance*. As Mandela and the opening quote by Calvin Coolidge illustrate, talent and ability alone are not sufficient. Persistence alone also is not enough. According to the equation, if either ability or persistence is absent then so is performance. As we will discuss, coupling your ability with persistence will provide you with an ongoing differentiator in life.

This simple but important research finding can readily be brought to life if you think back to high school. We all know of someone who was at or near the top of our graduating class in terms of grades; school came easily to that person. Yet it was surprising to learn years later—perhaps at a class reunion—that this same person had not been immensely successful after high school. It may have been even more surprising to learn that an average or somewhat below-average student had done very well in the years following graduation. In actuality, the different trajectories of these individuals should not have been surprising at all. The reason for the difference is typically quite clear. The former high performer based his career path on ability alone and was missing one of the key ingredients: persistence. The average student, however, had both of these ingredients.

Let's pretend that ability and persistence both can be scored on a 10-point scale (with 1 being low and 10 being high). The student who had the great grades was maybe a 9 on ability and a 5 on persistence, for an overall performance quotient of 45 (9×5). The average but ultimately more successful student was only a 6 on ability, but an 8 on persistence. This combination results in a performance quotient of 48 (6×8), which is higher than that of the student with the high grades. It is of course not this clean-cut in the real world, but it is easy enough for you to consider how this formula could apply to you and your trajectory at work. The point is not that you need to be a 10 on each element, but that you can compensate for lower ability if you are extremely persistent.

The elements underlying the significance of persistence are closely connected to motivation theory in psychology. Motivation, though, can be short-lived if the reasoning behind it is faulty. However, if you are motivated for the right reasons, it will become much easier to remain persistent, even when confronted with adversity. You have likely heard of *intrinsic* and *extrinsic* motivation. Persistence is accelerated when you apply yourself toward those things that you are intrinsically driven to achieve; that is, those things that you love doing.

The factors underlying intrinsic and extrinsic motivation are very different. On the one hand, extrinsic drive may get you jump-started on something, but it has a short shelf life. The reason is that extrinsic motivation is about external factors that make you want to do something, and you may not have any passion for what you are doing beyond a material reward you seek. For example, someone may offer you money to help build a start-up company, but if you do not believe in it and are not emotionally attached to the mission, you are likely to lose enthusiasm before long. It has been shown that extrinsic rewards will actually lead to what is known as an undermining effect on performance. More specifically, you become less likely to reach a goal when the only thing that motivates you toward it is a tangible reward.

On the other hand, intrinsic drive is about what excites you. It is what invigorates you and pushes you to do more. It is not about the extrinsic motivational factors like pay or other rewards. Extrinsic rewards are important (and often necessary) but alone do not independently create a high or sustained level of persistence. Only intrinsic motivation can do this. People often state that they would continue to do what they do even if there were no money involved. They say this because they truly love and are motivated by what they do. This is intrinsic motivation, and it is something you must seek in order to create a fulfilling trajectory.

A great example of intrinsic drive is found in professional skateboarder Tony Hawk. He grew up with a love for the sport during a time when it was considered something for outcasts. Nevertheless, he had such a passion and skill for skateboarding that he knew he had to chase his dream. He loved it so much that he pursued it knowing he would not make any money from it. He was intrinsically driven to be the best skateboarder in the world.

Hawk shows us how you can capitalize on your passions and intrinsic drive to develop opportunities where none existed. When he picked up his first skateboard he could not have imagined that he would have a video game named after him. He would not have believed that he could turn his skill into a business empire. A word Hawk uses to describe how he achieved his success is *authenticity*. Through being authentic you will do more than if you sell yourself and your principles short. And you cannot be fully authentic if you are not intrinsically connected to your goals.

Tony Hawk actually describes his trajectory in *How Did I Get Here?: The Ascent of an Unlikely CEO*. In it he relates how he received his first skateboard at the age of nine and could not get enough of it. How he turned pro at the age of fourteen. How one of his first checks was for just eighty-five cents! He then had a rapid jump in his trajectory and was making nearly $150,000 per year at the age of nineteen. Just a few years later he was back to barely making enough money to pay the rent. He began to realize that he needed to do more than just skate, but he did not want to let go of skating. What he found was a way to focus a business on his passion and build a brand around his name. This involved risk, and several times he had to invest nearly all of his money, including taking money out against his mortgage. Despite the challenges, he persisted and eventually ended up expanding his brand into areas as diverse as clothing, mobile phones, Happy Meal toys at McDonald's, and even bedding and roller coasters.

Tony had some luck along the way, particularly when ESPN introduced the X Games (at the time called Extreme Games) and highlighted him as one of the stars. He also had ability. And don't forget persistence. At those X Games he was still trying to become the first person in history to land a 900 (a skateboard trick that involves two and one-half full rotations in the air). During his run he ran out of time after eight consecutive failed attempts. Yet he kept trying, even though his attempts would not count toward the official competition. On his twelfth attempt the world saw him pull off the first successful 900. Had he not persisted it would not have happened. He found a way to blend his ability, persistence, and passion into a successful trajectory, just as you will be able to do.

RUN YOUR RACE

Like Tony Hawk, to maximize your success you must allow your passion and enthusiasm to aid you along your journey. Paradoxically, though, you can have too much or too little enthusiasm. What you should strive for is reaching a state of *balanced enthusiasm*. This is difficult when you are driven only by extrinsic factors, but much easier to obtain when you pursue something with intrinsic intentions.

The Yerkes-Dodson Law in psychology can be used to help explain this phenomenon. Researchers Robert Yerkes and John Dodson found that mice were able to most quickly learn which door to enter when moderate levels of stimulus were administered after a mistake (in this case an electrical shock was given). If the strength of the shock was too low or too high it took longer for the mice to learn to correctly discriminate between the door with a shock and the one without a shock. When the learning curves were flipped upside down, an inverted U-shape relationship was revealed between performance and the level of stimuli present.

Applied to work, this reveals that the proper level of enthusiasm—but not misplaced or over-the-top enthusiasm—is necessary in order to ensure optimal performance. If your enthusiasm level is too low you may lose some ability to concentrate, lose confidence, or even be fearful of the activity at hand. In Figure 2-1 you can see that when there is no enthusiasm there is no performance. When this occurs, persistence wanes. On the other end of the spectrum there is again no performance if enthusiasm is too high. This can occur because your decision making and reasoning become clouded and inhibit performance. In cases of extreme fear or panic a person's arousal is too high, which explains why people will often "freeze up" in certain situations. Similarly, doing something very basic may seem more difficult if you have a lot of pressure riding on the outcome. For example, professional golfers experience this when a two-foot putt is necessary to win a tournament. In that case the putt seems infinitely longer than it otherwise would.

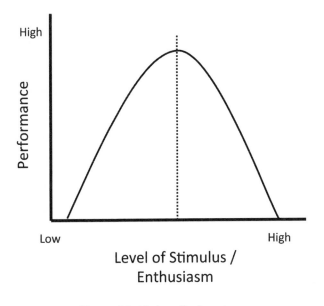

Figure 2-1: Yerkes-Dodson Law

You must therefore seek to find that optimal or balanced level of enthusiasm. Your performance will suffer when it is too high or too low. Even Tony Hawk realized that he had to move past some of his business ventures. Sure, he was enthusiastic about these but knew that he had to face reality and focus on ventures that had a greater chance of succeeding.

A note of caution is also in order related to this phenomenon. Enthusiasm and persistence are complementary, but you should not confuse the two. Enthusiasm is great, and can build excitement, but it has a much shorter shelf life than does persistence. Fans at a football game may be very enthusiastic, but it's hard to say they are persistent. The players, by contrast, must be persistent. Talent alone does not get most players to the National Football League. Players may not be enthusiastic about waking up at 5 a.m. to lift weights, but they persist in doing so. And doing so consistently over time is what differentiates them from hundreds of thousands of other athletes who had the same dream.

This is particularly true for complex tasks. When you are doing something that you are very familiar with—riding a bike, for example—you will likely not crash even if you are very excited. With a new or complex task, however, it is more important that you have the right level of arousal. Have you ever found yourself not able to sleep because your mind would not stop racing? Imagine trying to concentrate on learning a new activity or trying to memorize something with that same racing mind. It would be very difficult to do so. The right level of focus and concentration is necessary to make it easier for you to learn and build out new skills. If you have too little energy and enthusiasm you will fall somewhere to the left of the dotted line in Figure 2-1. If you have too much you will fall somewhere to the right. In both of these instances you will learn and do less than what you will be able to if you remain at your optimal level.

Marathon runners are a competitive group, and I have never met a marathoner who did not have a goal for the race. For some it is just to finish. For others it is to finish without stopping. For yet others it is to beat a certain time or even to win. If you have ever watched a marathon you might have been surprised at the number of people who were walking before the second mile or even during the first. Surely they had trained and were prepared to run farther without stopping. The Yerkes-Dodson Law can be used to explain why this happens to runners who are so physically well trained.

At the beginning of each race hundreds and often thousands of people take off at one time, all with the same overarching goal: to finish the race in the best time possible. During the start, superfluous enthusiasm and competitive comparison with nearby runners can overtake persistence, which leads to a devastating outcome. Instead of sticking with a plan and persisting with it for the full race, runners will get caught up with the pace of others who are faster and mistakenly try to keep up. As someone who has participated in a marathon, I can attest firsthand to how many people are "gassed" after less than a mile and are soon left walking because they tried to run too fast out of the gate. This aligns with what is expected from the Yerkes-Dodson Law. At the beginning of the race those runners with over-the-top enthusiasm started too fast and were left with diminished performance against their original expectations. In the Yerkes-Dodson model they fall to the right of the dotted line.

Keeping this principle in mind will enable you to "run your race" at work. If you have a plan, be cautious if you decide to abruptly deviate from it and extend yourself into an area in which you are not likely to succeed. In race terms, you may be able to run a few seven-minute miles, but if you trained and were prepared to run nine-minute miles, no amount of persistence will compensate. At work, then, strategically deviate from your race when opportunities arise, but be sure to remember what it is you are trying to accomplish.

GET OUT OF YOUR OWN WAY

According to the results from an annual survey conducted by the American Psychological Association (APA), the number one barrier to success that people report is willpower. Yet 71 percent of the same respondents felt this was something they could learn to improve and do better. Turned another way, nearly three-quarters of people think they can control the one area that they feel is the biggest obstacle preventing them from reaching their goals. This takes us back to the performance equation. You cannot entirely change your ability, but you have much more control of your willpower and how strongly you persist toward your goals.

If you believe you can reach something and persist toward it, you will have an advantage over the 71 percent of the people who believe that this is what is preventing them from achieving their goals. It could be something as basic as losing weight, or it could be something as complex as revolutionizing an industry. Both of these are less likely without persistence. All meaningful accomplishments are less likely without persistence.

At the same time you need to be pragmatic and wise in your pursuits. Persistence is an important and admirable trait. *Blind persistence*, however, is not. You must be realistic with those things that you seek to accomplish. No amount of persistence is going to make you golf as well as Tiger Woods or play basketball like LeBron James. Regardless of how persistent you are, you will not be able to jump over a river that is thirty feet wide. But if you take a step back and reconsider your goal—in this case, to get to the other side—you can devise a new plan. In doing so you persist in gathering the materials necessary to build a bridge to the other side and reach your goal. The point is that persistence necessitates reevaluation. Without rethinking your strategy and approach you may be persisting in a fruitless endeavor. What you can do is be as good as possible against the standard you set for yourself as you reach for your trajectory.

Persistence also requires preparation. The Roman philosopher Seneca, who lived more than 2,000 years ago, is credited with saying, "Luck is where the crossroads of opportunity and preparation meet." Despite the passage of time and the exponentially more complex world in which we live and work, this reasoning still applies. When opportunity arises you will become your own enemy if you have not prepared for it in advance. If you want something you must treat it as an eventuality. You must believe that it will happen. And when it does you must enter the situation knowing that you have done everything within your power to seize that moment, which will leave you in a state or readiness when it occurs. Doing this will give you comfort, knowing you have left no effort or regrets behind.

RANGE RESTRICTION

Most companies have hiring processes that in some way attempt to identify the top candidates for open positions so that they can choose the people most likely to be successful. Assuming you and others have gone through a similar hiring process, you will be in a work environment that is impacted by what statisticians refer to as *range restriction*. When range restriction occurs, there is less variability on some known factor(s). If this factor happens to be ability, you and others at work will be similar on the first half of the performance equation we discussed earlier in this chapter. This means that you must focus on ensuring that you have the necessary differentiating persistence to enable you to stand out from and outperform the others. Whereas they may give up, you must persist—even if just slightly more—to achieve even greater things.

Research in the business world strongly supports the assertion that persistence is a desirable—and differentiating—characteristic of successful leaders. Steven Kaplan of the University of Chicago Booth School of Business sought to test this proposition using data from more than 300 candidates for CEO roles in private equity and venture capitalist firms. The candidates were all assessed on five primary areas: leadership, personal, intellectual, interpersonal, and persistence. What is unique about this study is that not only were the candidates assessed before they were hired, but the researchers were then able to use this information to help identify the characteristics most responsible for future success among the CEOs. Along with efficiency and being proactive, persistence was one of the three most important factors in determining the performance of the CEOs and their companies. This shows us that even at the highest levels of an organization—where most everyone likely has above-average ability—

persistence emerges as the differentiating factor in determining success.

You may ask, What about the importance of persistence if you are not a CEO? It still applies. If we go to the other end of the spectrum we find the same thing with children. In *How Children Succeed: Grit, Curiosity, and the Hidden Power of Character,* Paul Tough discusses what leads children to succeed over time. One of the essential elements he uncovered was persistence, which can be a core part of each person's character. What's important to note is that ability (intelligence) is somewhat predetermined. Nutrition, health, and other factors can help, but there is only so much of an opportunity to change this somewhat innate factor once you reach adulthood. Persistence, remember, is much more under your control.

This is of particular relevance when you consider the many differences in our backgrounds and childhoods. On the one hand, consider an individual from a broken family with a low income. She may have a more difficult path and trajectory to achieve success, but can do so given ability and persistence. On the other hand, consider someone from a family of considerable wealth and prestige. He will have great opportunities and access to resources that should make success easier. Yet despite great ability this person does not amount to much. Why? Because he took things for granted and chose not to persist with his self-improvement. Whether it is children, CEOs, or you, persistence matters, and it matters all the time.

PATIENT URGENCY

Persistence includes an element of time, and therefore one of
its essential attributes is patience. Without patience you cannot embody persistence. These intertwined attributes can ensure that you do not do too much too quickly as you progress
through your charted trajectory. Unfortunately blind persistence results in patience going out the window. Companies
that experience early success often become too enamored
with growth and then become numb to caution and patience.

Take Boston Market, which at one point was one of the
fastest-growing food chains in the United States. It had its eye
on a great amount of growth and put together a plan for
rapid expansion. The growth strategy quickly became a
doomed proposition because Boston Market did not seek out
persistent but patient growth. Instead of focusing on the right
rate of growth, it focused on rapid growth. At its peak Boston Market had more than 900 restaurants. It then went
through bankruptcy and had to close nearly 200 stores after
it had overexpanded. The main problem was that the leaders
of the company were so focused on growth that they
overlooked sound business principles such as developing good
leaders and building community relationships. They lost sight
of the building blocks and practices that had made the
organization successful in the beginning. With your career
you must not make the mistake of losing the essence of who
you are and what you have sought to accomplish.

In-N-Out Burger, which was recently named by *Consumer Reports* as the best fast-food restaurant chain in the

United States, has taken the opposite approach to growth. Its founders knew early on that rapid growth could be damaging to the chain. They instead decided to be patient but persistent with their growth. The chain's founder, Harry Snyder, resisted the temptation to take the company public or to expand using a franchise model. By deliberately choosing to maintain only company-managed restaurants, In-N-Out Burger took a different approach than did most fast-food chains. When pressure for growth is high, franchising provides a way to quickly generate revenue. While doing this can increase revenue in the short term, it results in lessened control of operations and can create greater risk in the long term. In adopting a franchise model the trajectory of the chain becomes less under leadership's control. As you plot your own trajectory you too should be careful to not give up control in areas that are important to you. You might experience a short-term gain, but the purpose of plotting your trajectory is to put in place a plan for sustained performance.

Comparing the different strategies taken by Boston Market and In-N-Out Burger reveals something inherently important about patience: Patience does not mean laziness or lack of urgency. It does, however, mean that you can strategically wait for the right opportunities. In-N-Out Burger focused on the right growth and ensuring that it had the capability for growth. For example, the company made a conscious decision to never expand faster than it had talent available to fill restaurant manager roles. In doing so it realized that persistence and patience would in the long run provide a more stable organization. Whether it is building your own skills or making decisions for an entire organization, you can learn from these examples in order to avoid making the same mistakes.

Being patient does not mean you should take your time and wait for things to come to you. It's just the opposite. You still need to have a sense of urgency about what you do. It is just that if you are impatient a host of negative outcomes can follow. For example, impatience is associated with expressing feelings of negativity, cynicism, and even disdain for others and their decision-making processes. By expressing a sense of *patient urgency* you will convey to others the importance of what you are doing. If you become unduly impatient you also run the risk of being perceived by others as unreasonable, bossy, and even selfish. When this occurs you are apt to lose support from others, which could be a great detriment to your career, as such support is often critical to obtaining success in any endeavor.

LEARNING FROM NAVY SEALS

A river shows great persistence over time as the water flows and continues to carve out a path. As time passes, this path can widen and become magnificent, but it does not happen overnight. Emulate a river with your persistence and seek out the path that is right for you and your goals. Doing this in order to stay on your trajectory will not always be easy, because we all encounter obstacles. As Ben Saunders learned (see "Getting Started" at the beginning of this book), head-winds may slow you down, but you must not let that resistance stop you from dreaming big and working toward achieving your goals. Persistence is what will allow you to reach the top, even while others become frustrated and decide to give up.

In *Lone Survivor*, Marcus Luttrell describes the grueling process people go through to become Navy SEALs. The SEALs are world renowned for their diverse skills and ability to withstand extreme situations and conditions. They explicitly call out the importance of perseverance and include this statement in their credo: "I will never quit. I persevere and thrive on adversity. My Nation expects me to be physically harder and mentally stronger than my enemies. If knocked down, I will get back up, every time." Many people may think that Navy SEALs are selected based on their physical prowess. This is partially true. However, what really differentiates them is their persistence and mental fortitude.

The ability to persist through nearly intolerable exercises is what really matters. Luttrell recalls that many of the strongest and most ferocious-looking candidates were often among the quickest to fail. Though they looked the part, they did not have the resilience necessary to make it through the program. During his Basic Underwater Demolition / SEALs (BUD/S) training 164 people were in his original cohort. Thirty-two made it through the trials. Luttrell states that he doesn't know how he made it through many parts, but credits willpower for keeping him going.

An examination of the Navy SEALs reveals that not only can you develop your persistence over time, but you can make it a core part of who you are. What they exemplify is positive effort. The boot camp instructors all know that those who have the drive and mental fortitude will put in the required effort to make it through the tests.

Jerry Rice, the all-time leading receiver in the NFL, also realized that persistence and effort were necessary to differentiate himself from others. He is similarly renowned for his grueling hill workouts, but he did not get there all at once. He got to the top of the hill step by step. And he continued the workouts during the offseason when so many other players were taking a break. He realized that if he could fight and persist against the hill during the offseason, he could do the same against his more tired opponents during the fourth quarter of a game.

At work you can follow the example of the Navy SEALs trials, Jerry Rice, and many other success stories. Your persistence can be what differentiates you from the other "best athletes" you are up against.

CONCLUSION

In many ways persistence can be tied back to Aesop's fable The Tortoise and the Hare. In the fable Aesop says, "A Hare one day ridiculed the short feet and slow pace of the Tortoise, who replied, laughing: 'Though you be swift as the wind, I will beat you in a race.' . . . The Tortoise never for a moment stopped, but went on with a slow but steady pace straight to the end of the course." There are two lessons within this fable. The first applies to the hare, who quickly found that overconfidence—and underestimating your competition—is not a wise move. The second, relating to the tortoise, is that persistence can enable you to overcome great odds and challenges.

No one doubts for a second that a hare is faster than a tortoise, but let's put the Ability × Persistence = Performance equation against this fable. The hare had the ability (A = 9), but did not persist on a high level (P= 3). Although the tortoise had lesser ability (A = 3), it had extreme persistence (P = 10). Though it was extremely close, the tortoise won the race, just as the formula would predict (expected performance = 30 for the tortoise versus 27 for the hare).

Of course none of this should be construed to mean that you should not move quickly. As we will discuss in Lesson 3, you must. But you must also not burn out or move so quickly that, like the hare, you think you cannot lose. When, like the tortoise, you persist, you don't give up. You certainly should not give up when your goal is attainable and still desirable to you.

One of the greatest things about persistence is that it is not going away. It is not a fad. It is not a commodity whose value will decline. Persistence will continue to stand the test of time as a differentiating characteristic that the most successful people possess. Sporting goods companies are even trying to measure persistence in athletic endeavors. Under Armour has even released a product that is designed to assess the wearer's persistence when exercising: It's a watch that measures willpower using a mathematical algorithm that calculates a score between one and ten.

Whether during exercise, at work, in your personal life, or anywhere else, persistence has been and will continue to be one of the most important factors for you to consider when plotting and working to attain your trajectory.

And here is an exercise to complete before the next lesson.

EXERCISE

Think for a moment about a goal that seems so easy, but has continually eluded you. We all have some of these. Maybe it's losing weight, completing a 5K race, or even learning a new language. Write the goal in the space provided on the Notes page and then list the reasons why has it eluded you. Was it because you did not persist in the face of difficulty and challenges? Did you give up too soon? It's time to change that. Dust off that goal. How far along did you make it last time when you stopped? Why did you stop or give up? Write down the answers to those questions on the Notes page. Then share your goal with others and tell them how far you are going to get this time (ideally all the way to your goal). When you feel ready to give up, persist. Reach out for support to the people you told. Do not stop where you stopped before. Go at least one—and preferably many—steps further this time. Remember, this is about persistence, and persistence is not easy.

NOTES

THINK BIG, ACT SMALL, MOVE QUICK

Go as far as you can see; when you get there,
you'll be able to see farther.

—J. P. MORGAN

Building and managing your trajectory involves putting in place a series of manageable steps and goals. Some of these steps, though critical to your ultimate goals and trajectory, may actually be rather small in nature. This should not be construed to mean that grand thinking is not desirable. In fact, it is just the opposite. Big thinking is critical. It just does not normally transpire overnight or by accident. In this lesson you will learn that you must think long-term, but the best path to reach your big goals is often through small actions and quick moves.

Take the home run hitter in baseball. He is fun to watch, because there is a chance that he might hit a big home run, but more frequently he will not. Success for a home run hitter might be getting a hit once every four at-bats, and a home run every ten at-bats. In contrast, the job of a lead-off hitter is to get on base. This difference is at the heart of the Think Big, Act Small, Move Quick strategy. Think big = win the game; act small = get on base in order to score a run; move quick = do it in the first inning, and steal second base to get into scoring position. In doing this, the lead-off hitter maximizes his (and the team's) chance of success, but does not close the door on a big home run every now and again.

In the final and deciding game seven of the 1967 World Series, Bob Gibson was the starting pitcher for the St. Louis Cardinals. He had won two games earlier in the series and picked up where he left off by continuing his pitching dominance in this game. But he did something else: he hit his big home run. His goal never varied—win the game, and do it batter by batter—but his approach and preparation led him to become one of the very few pitchers to ever hit a home run in the World Series. For context, over the course of his career he hit a home run in fewer than 2 percent of his regular season at-bats. Over the course of three World Series he hit a home run in more than 7 percent of his at-bats! What this also illustrates is that not only does a think big, act small, move quick strategy set up victories every day, it also puts you in a position to do so when the stakes are the highest.

There are many examples of people who reached unbelievable heights one small goal at a time, including another well-known instance from the baseball world. On September 6, 1995, Cal Ripken Jr. played in his 2,131st consecutive major league baseball game, breaking the record Lou Gehrig had held for fifty-six years. Ripken of course did this over the course of many years. In a way, he had set 2,131 interim goals on the way to the record. For Ripken, what started as a rather simple goal evolved over time into what became a grand goal. The first goal of Ripken's baseball career was undoubtedly not to break the consecutive games streak, but more simply to make the team and be successful. Early in his career the idea of breaking the record was likely not even a blip on his radar. Eventually the streak came into focus as his number of consecutive games grew over time. Remember this: As you grow in your career you need to keep your eyes open to new and even previously unthought-of goals that present themselves. What once seemed unimaginable will very quickly become quite realistic as you follow your plan.

Similarly, Emmitt Smith—the National Football League's all-time leading rusher—describes in his autobiography how it was actually many small goals that led to his record-setting 18,355 career rushing yards. In every game he set a goal to rush for at least four yards per carry. While he did not reach this every single game, he persevered and would then look to get even more yards the next time. Or think back to Ben Saunders, whose story we discussed in the "Getting Started" chapter of this book. During his expedition to the North Pole he always kept his focus on what was in front of him. He continually broke his quest into little chunks by focusing on reaching the next piece of ice, and the next piece. Through these building steps he reached his goal and covered the full 1,240-mile journey. He thought big with his plan of reaching the North Pole. He started small with each step and chunk of ice. He moved as quick as conditions would safely allow, but no faster. In any endeavor, attempting too much too quickly is a recipe for disaster. Along his journey no individual step was grandiose, but collectively each step led to what was a record-breaking feat. Like Bob Gibson, Cal Ripken Jr., Emmitt Smith, and Ben Saunders, everyone has an inherent desire to be successful. Leveraging think big, act small, move quick will help you in your pursuit.

Applied to work, these examples prove that if you continually play in game after game, and are accumulating base hits, you not only are moving the needle forward, you are setting up a situation where you will also hit home runs. This is a powerful combination. All three elements of think Big, act Small, move Quick (BSQ) must work together for you. The world has no shortage of big ideas; it is short on big ideas that people actually carry out to fruition. Viewing your think big goals through the daily lens of acting small but moving quickly will allow you to realize your goals.

REACH YOUR SUMMITS

History is littered with innovators and explorers who decided to think big and aspire to do something that nobody else had done before them. Mountain climbing is one of the most arduous yet gratifying endeavors for many such adventurers. Scattered across the globe are what are known as the Seven Summits, which consist of the highest mountain on each continent. Despite the highest mountain (Mt. Everest) being successfully scaled in 1953, it was not until more than thirty years later that a single person was able to climb each of the Seven Summits.

This feat was accomplished by the most unlikely of individuals, someone who was not a natural mountaineer. Dick Bass was a fifty-one-year-old businessman with little climbing experience; few would have believed that this white-collar executive would end up being the first person to attain such a significant accomplishment. To do so he had to think big, act small (though in this case "small" was each mountain!), and move quick. "Quick" was particularly important because of seasonal climbing windows for some of the peaks, not to mention the fact that at least one other climber was also trying to become the first to climb each of the mountains.

To reach such a bold goal took great preparation and training. Bass's "think big" was to climb all of the mountains: his "act small" was to prepare for and tackle one mountain at a time, and his "move quick" was to accomplish his mission before his window of time was over or someone beat him to it. 22,835 feet. 20,320 feet. 19,340 feet. 18,481 feet. 16,067 feet. 7,316 feet. 29,029 feet. These are the elevations of each of the seven mountains in the order that Bass climbed them, and it is another way of illustrating that successful trajectories are not always constant.

In his case he actually went downward through the mountain elevations until he reached his final—and highest—summit at the top of Mt. Everest. He started with Aconcagua in South America, then McKinley (Denali) in North America, followed by Kilimanjaro in Africa. He then turned to El'brus in Europe, Vinson in Antarctica, and Kosciusko in Australia, before finishing with a successful summit of Mt. Everest in Asia. He did not start with the smallest and then work his way up; instead he followed the plan he had put together to maximize his chances of reaching his trajectory. The numbers, though, do not convey the failure and persistence along the way. It actually was not until Bass's fourth attempt that he succeeded in climbing Mt. Everest. So while he failed three times, he continued to persist and was able to reach his ultimate trajectory. Bass reminds us of Lesson 2: It is persistence that is the real differentiator when situations are most difficult.

Like Dick Bass you will find that it pays for you to think big when you consider what you want to achieve. No matter how hard you try you will never be able to do everything at once. Over time, though, you will be able to accomplish that which you seek, by tackling one mountain at a time. Each mountain will come with challenges, but when you break these into the respective pieces it will become easier for you to meet and overcome each one—and to do so quickly.

GOAL MANAGEMENT

All of this sounds good, but how do you actually go about it? A critical element of BSQ that enables this to happen is to set goals that serve as guideposts along your trajectory. This is supported by goal-setting theory, which is one of the foundations of organizational psychology. Though there have been thousands of studies on goal setting, the body of work as it relates to individual performance can be summarized quite simply through a few distinctions:

1. A goal is better than no goal.
2. A specific goal is better than a broad goal.
3. A hard and specific goal is better than an easy goal.

If you make it a practice to routinely establish goals you will have covered the primary tenet of goal theory. And if you make your goals specific (e.g., "become a partner in my law firm by the end of next year" versus "be successful at work") you have then knocked out the second tenet. Now you get to the more complex part of setting goals. The research is clear: difficult but attainable goals will consistently result in the most success. This has been an enduring finding that has been replicated in countless settings. On the one hand, if you set goals that are too difficult the goal becomes unrealistic and you lose motivation and fail to achieve it. On the other hand, if you set a goal that is too easy you will have no problem reaching it, but in doing so you may settle for something less than your best effort and thereby miss out on what could have been a more profound accomplishment. If in your career and life you only set goals that are easy, you will shortchange yourself and thereby not reach your true limits. You therefore must find an optimal balance of what is hard but realistic versus realistic but too easy.

A second part of this is determining the right time horizon for your goals. This is known as *goal proximity*. If you set a goal that is too distal (far in the future), you will reduce your chance of reaching it. More specifically, proximal (near-term) goals, which you can set as part of move quick, are more likely to be achieved than are distal goals. Because they are by nature shorter term, proximal goals tend to be smaller than bigger goals. As an example, a proximal goal at the start of the year might be *develop restaurant business and opening strategy by June.* A more distal goal would be opening the restaurant. Through attaining one proximal goal after another you accomplish two very important things: 1) You move closer to your ultimate goal; 2) You succeed in these and in turn continue to grow your confidence in your abilities. Bear in mind that proximal goals will continue to evolve as you progress. When you start a project at work, for instance, what was once a very distal goal will become a proximal goal as you move through the milestones of the initiative.

By setting goals and focusing on proximal and interim goals you will find that you are giving yourself something else that we've learned is so important: feedback (Lesson 1). As you progress you will either succeed or fail. Either of these outcomes will let you know what worked and what did not. You will feel progression, and in doing so you will gain more self-efficacy. By now you should be beginning to realize how all of your actions are interconnected. Each little success will create a stronger mindset and prepare you for more success, which will in turn make you inclined to persist even harder in the pursuit of your goals.

Weight loss is a commonly used example of how to set goals. If you think about losing weight but never set an actual goal, it is unlikely to happen. If you decide broadly, "I want to lose twelve pounds," you will likely lose less weight than if you set a specific goal to lose one pound every month for a year. If you really want to lose five pounds, but only set a goal to lose one pound, you will likely stop there. By setting a goal of five pounds you will undoubtedly achieve more. Even losing just one additional pound would actually constitute a 100 percent improvement over losing only one pound.

You can similarly leverage goal-setting principles in your career to help guide your trajectory. As you chart your trajectory you must consider the importance of ensuring that you set goals that are specific and attainable yet difficult. If you have no goals it will be very hard to have any idea of what you need to work on. If you have a broad goal, such as wanting to open a business, you won't know where to start. If you have an easy goal, you run the risk of selling yourself short. You therefore need to create a plan that includes a series of goals. If you wanted to open a restaurant, for example, you might start with the plan shown in Table 3-1.

Deciding to open a successful restaurant is an example of thinking big. Wrapping a one-year time frame around it will underscore the need for you to move quickly. Each of the goals in Table 3-1 can be viewed as a guidepost that can be considered part of act small, but each of these goals is very important. In fact, you would likely fail if you missed any of these act small goals. Moreover, each of these when considered individually becomes more manageable and allows you to tackle realistic yet difficult tasks in pursuit of your goal. Hopefully you can see that breaking it down in this manner

Table 3-1. Think Big, Act Small, Move Quick Plan

Think Big	Act Small	Move Quick
Open a successful restaurant within one year	Develop business strategy	By June
	Decide on business name	By July
	Obtain financing	By August
	Finalize restaurant location and sign lease	By September
	Begin interior remodel and construction	September 15
	Hire lead chef	October
	Develop menu	By end of the year
	Hire and train staff	January–February
	Grand opening	March 15 at 6 p.m.

would make it much easier for you to stay on track than would simply setting a goal to open a restaurant. And when you move quickly you will navigate through all of the goals that lead up to opening the restaurant. You can now see how this all builds and can work together.

Let's now put this lesson in the context of the early stages of a career. Perhaps you're a recent college graduate who as-

his is great, but how
everaged to help you
milestone goals and
ing each one. By de-
adily progressing to-
reatly improve your
ay becoming CEO. If
will more likely end
up becoming overly reliant on luck and chasing an amor-
phous aspiration.

Regardless of your career stages, goals can be used to
guide your development. It is hard to get a job without a plan
to get there. Goals can be used to frame the plan you need to
put in place to ensure that you obtain the experiences you
need to prepare for your next job. Within this you can also
create goal targets for areas in which you need development
to improve your skills. Maybe it is taking a course on strategic
leadership, or seeking an opportunity to work on a project in
a different function. Regardless of what specific actions align
with your needs, putting goals in place will make it easier for
you to hold yourself accountable for reaching them.

SMALL BITES

As you learned in Lesson 2, patience is critical to your success and is an essential element of the think big, act small,
move quick strategy. Unfortunately, patience can be hard to
master and is one of those traits that tend to improve with
age. When you use the move quick approach you will find

that you are continually able to make incremental progress toward your larger goals. These "small bites" will make it easier for you to manage obstacles along the path to a grand goal. In doing so you can avoid making sloppy mistakes or overreaching. At the same time, when you split up your goals and trajectory with this approach, it can seem that progress does not happen fast enough. This is not the case.

Evolutionary thoughts and progress will result in revolutionary accomplishment, and you will be amazed at how rapidly this can actually transpire. As your successes continue to build you will feel that you are moving quickly along the path to your goals. On the other hand, if you are at step one and your goal is to reach step ten it may seem that you are walking in place if you have no other steps pre-specified along your path. If you have sub-goals for steps two through nine it will seem that you are moving so much faster. Many of us can relate to a long road trip that you chunk up into various milestones. This process follows the same principle. A ten-hour trip might have a bathroom break at two hours, a countdown to the halfway point at five hours, a food stop at seven hours, etc., and then all of a sudden the trip seems to have moved along much faster than it otherwise would.

There is a classic psychological study by Walter Mischel of Stanford University in which children were each given a marshmallow to eat. They were told, however, that if they waited fifteen minutes before eating the marshmallow, they would be given a second one. Seems simple enough, with no long-term impact, correct? Turns out this experiment and its implications are not as simple as they might initially seem. Mischel followed these children for many years to track their subsequent progress in life. As time went by, the children who had resisted the initial temptation to eat the first marsh-mallow were found to have higher SAT scores and were more successful in their careers. Something as basic as delaying gratification for fifteen minutes actually mattered.

Imagine that for a second. The simple delayed gratifica-tion of waiting to eat a marshmallow was found to reliably predict success later in life. Eating the marshmallow immedi-ately would have been easy—and fulfilling—but choosing to wait fifteen minutes resulted in something even more fulfill-ing because a second marshmallow would then be given. Keeping this in mind will benefit you throughout your life and career. The gratifying dessert you eat now will lead to a need for more exercise later. The shortcut you opted to take at work will lead to needless errors found later. Saying some-thing off the cuff that gives you momentary satisfaction will be something you regret later. Many people choose to eat the first marshmallow as soon as possible at every point in their careers. Doing so can result in taking new jobs solely for immediate tangible gain but will not enhance your portfolio of experiences. By waiting you can eat the right marshmallow at the right time. Move quick, but be patient in making the right moves. Do not move for the sake of moving. And do not mistake activity for purposeful action and meaningful pro-gress. It's important to move quick, but it still needs to be the right move.

DISTRACTED DECISION MAKING

The brain is amazing, and new findings continue to emerge demonstrating how powerful it really is. We rarely think about thinking, but despite this the brain continues to do so for us. Recent research from Carnegie Mellon University has uncovered a very interesting finding in this area. It supports the importance of the "move quick" aspect of this strategy by underscoring that overthinking decisions can lead to sub-optimal outcomes. When you overanalyze something, you not only can become stressed and confused, you also lose valuable time.

What the researchers found was that decision making can actually be improved under conditions in which individuals are distracted. They found that by distracting people from the decision at hand, the subsequent decisions were better. This finding was discovered during an experiment in which the researchers shared features of four different cars with people, and then gave some of them a task for a few minutes to distract them from thinking about which car was the best option.

Based on the results of the brain imaging, the researchers noticed that the portion of the brain that was processing the information continued to remain activated and learn, even while the person was engaged in a different task. This suggests that you can let your brain process complex information even when you are not thinking about it. This unconscious activity can lead to better decision making.

When you think too much about something you can get lost in the volume of data and options, which leads to paralysis by analysis. Your indecision then becomes a decision because you fail to decide in a fast enough manner how to proceed. The results lend scientific support to the "go with your gut" model of decision making. Do not overthink issues. If you find yourself overwhelmed or confused by something, stop overanalyzing it. Sleep on it or go do something else and then make the decision when your mind is freed up.

This is further supported by a classic decision-making study that looked at specifying the thought processes connected to the reasons behind choices that people made. In the experiment the authors asked people to taste and rate jams. Those who did so quickly had ratings very similar to those of expert tasters. The participants in another group were asked to provide the reasons for their ratings. When they did this they began to overthink and change their decisions, which resulted in very little similarity to the choices of the expert raters. But this was with jam. Would it also apply in a more high-stakes decision-making scenario? To check this the authors conducted a second study in which students had to make decisions about courses to take for their upcoming sophomore year. As with the first study, the students who were asked to justify their selections chose inferior options. Overthinking once again led to less effective decision making.

The need to make fast decisions does not mean you should make rash decisions. You still need to base your decisions on logic and sound reasoning. However, when you are torn between multiple options, do not ruminate for too long. You likely already know the right answer and are simply spending time trying to find more supporting evidence. If you are at this point, you need to make a decision and move on. If you do not do so, others will move on, and move out in front of you.

Intel learned this the hard way. Intel is famous for the computer memory chips that it developed and that became the backbone of its business in the early 1980s. Yet it is memory chips that could have put the company out of business. Why? Because the company hung on to them as its core business for too long, when what they needed at the time was a decisive decision to expand into other areas. As Japanese competitors flooded the market with cheaper—and better—alternatives, Intel's profit in this area began to decline. Many other companies in this line of products went out of business as a result, and Intel was nearly one of them. However, after a candid conversation in 1985 with Gordon Moore, Intel's chairman and CEO at the time, Andy Grove (who would succeed Moore as CEO) decided that it was time to let go of memory chips and move on to microprocessors.

The path to this decision was quite straightforward, even if the path from that point on was very difficult. During the conversation Grove asked Moore what would happen if they lost their jobs and a new management team were brought in. Without hesitation Moore stated that a new team would move Intel out of the memory chip business. In hindsight this may seem obvious, but at the time it was asking a business to turn its back on what had been its foundation and identity as a company. Moore knew, however, that it had to be done to not only survive, but to grow to an even better place.

At that point memory chips were so central to the business that thousands of employees were dedicated to creating them. In total, more than 7,000 employees were laid off as Intel moved development and production away from memory and toward microprocessors. Had a decision been made earlier, a more gradual—and potentially less disruptive—transition could have been made. Grove estimated that the turnaround took about ten years to accomplish.

With the pace of change occurring in many industries, your decision-making frame of reference is more important than ever. As the speed of change increases, the need to move quick rises as well. If you are in a slow-moving industry you may have a bit more time, but nevertheless, do not rest for long. Let's consider this in the context of your industry. If you work in the railroad industry, for instance, you may be able to spend more time processing major decisions and potential changes in direction. If you are with an Internet start-up company or stock brokerage, however, waiting an equivalent amount of time can easily lead to missing out on a major opportunity.

In the technology sector the speed of the industry is tremendous and is a factor that must be considered in decision making. Your decision-making frame of reference can be viewed along a continuum based on the speed of industry and the size of the problem at hand. These factors will help guide how quickly you must move with your decisions. Figure 3-1 illustrates the fact that as the pace of your industry quickens,

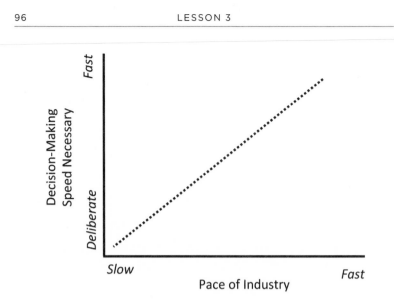

Figure 3-1: Decision-Making Slope

so too must your ability to make quick decisions. You must be aware that the pace of industry is not static. Whereas technology continues to move at breakneck speed as a whole, certain segments will slow down, while others will accelerate.

Consider Internet browsers. While these continue to evolve and improve, the speed of innovation has stabilized compared to when they were introduced. But other areas are moving faster than ever, and decision-making delays must be avoided. I think one of the most fascinating inventions ever is the 3D printer. When I first began to read about the concept (and I now wish I would have bought stock right then) it was hard to fathom that such a technology was even possible. It was surreal to imagine that you could send something in a manner similar to an e-mail or fax and then thousands of miles away a solid object would be generated. The range of uses runs from simple things like creating plastic prototypes to more complex projects such as building cars and generating organs for human use, and even more futuristic thinking such as applying this technology to build command posts on the moon or even Mars! This exemplifies thinking ahead and adapting to changing conditions and capabilities. I am not suggesting that you need to invent the next technology that changes the world, but you do need to recognize that you cannot always dwell on decisions for too long. Because the uses of 3D printing are so vast, it is not entirely clear how this ability will be fully leveraged. What is clear is that those who move the quickest will have the greatest advantage in this new market space.

MILITARY PRECEDENCE

Top military leaders are very adept at using the principles of think big, act small, move quick. Napoleon Bonaparte, who is widely regarded as one of the most successful military leaders in history, leveraged this principle when he sought to use military might to relentlessly expand the footprint of France. In what is regarded as one of the most profound military campaigns in history, Napoleon led his troops to victory at the Battle of Austerlitz. During the battle he cemented victory over an alliance against France that consisted of Austria,

Great Britain, Sweden, and Russia. This group of countries, collectively known as the Third Coalition, was the last major barrier to Napoleon and France obtaining nearly full European dominance.

When you consider the path that Napoleon followed to victory, you will notice that he leveraged the principles of think big, act small, move quick. Over a period of roughly twenty years he waged countless battles, involving millions of troops. Napoleon utilized speed and flexibility as a main tactic as much as possible. He was notorious for requiring his troops to make difficult marches of great distances in extreme conditions in order to reach the enemy at a place of his choosing. Doing so kept his adversaries guessing and enabled him to create an element of surprise.

One of the great aspects of being decisive is that it allows you to remain on the cutting edge. Others will spend time trying to catch up and figuring out what you are going to do next. They will look to you as a leader. You too must begin to think in this way. When you identify up front what your goals are, you can build your career strategy around them. Beyond recognizing the need to act quickly on the battlefield when the stakes were the highest, Napoleon also knew the importance of doing the same for personal career decisions. At one point early in his trajectory he was purportedly given three minutes in which to decide to accept a new military command. He accepted and from there launched one of the most chronicled military careers in history.

The ability to make quick and effective decisions—particularly under difficult situations or when the stakes are high—is a hallmark of successful leaders. Looking back on their careers, rarely do leaders profess that they regret making a mistake, unless the mistake was not acting quickly enough. Most leaders in retrospect will say that they regret the decisions they did not make fast enough. If they would have made faster decisions they would have been able to capitalize on more opportunities. You will have one large decision to make (think big) and then will need to make many small but quick decisions (move fast) along the way.

SMALL STEPS ARE BIG STEPS

All three elements of think big, act small, move quick must work together for you. As you move forward you should remember that your capabilities are only as good as your ability to execute. Many people have the capability to succeed, but fall short on execution. This failing is largely based on people not having a clear and realistic plan. The result is overshooting and trying to do too much at once, thereby doing nothing well. This is not to imply that you should not take risks. Small steps do not necessarily mean small risk. If all you take are average risks, you will likely obtain average results. The real magic is in identifying risk and then taking the right size steps to mitigate it.

In his book *Little Bets*, Peter Sims discusses the idea that smaller incremental progress serves as a stepping-stone for extraordinary breakthroughs. By tackling these little bets, Sims states, you allow yourself to learn quickly. Whether the learning leads to success or failure, you can use that information to recalibrate and plan your next step forward. As stated at the outset of this book, success rarely happens overnight. When you think of a little bet, you think about something that you would like to attain, but that in and of itself seldom will be life-changing. However, as you continue to amass victories through a series of little bets, you will see great change in your life. In addition, little bets—like proximal goals—serve another critical function. They act as a reward and build the self-efficacy that is so important. The rewards then become a motivator to persist even further.

In more practical terms, let's consider again a goal to lose weight through dieting. Successful dieters are experts at this approach. A dieter thinks big with an overall weight-loss goal, starts with small initial goals (the little bets), and doesn't delay in beginning the necessary efforts. People often like to brag about going on a diet and talk about how much weight they plan to lose. This seems insignificant, but is incredibly important. Telling others about your goals can actually increase your likelihood of reaching them. When you tell others, you are creating an implicit contract that you do not want to break. People have a general dislike of telling others that they did not follow through on something. The moment you tell someone about a goal, you have just strengthened your commitment to yourself, and created a type of contract with the person.

CONCLUSION

When you follow the BSQ approach along your trajectory you will feel yourself gaining momentum. You will feel that something that seemed quite difficult is actually very manageable. You will have the confidence to get there. Your accomplishments will grow, as will your belief in yourself. As this transpires you will find that you are almost unknowingly thinking bigger and bigger as you take on new challenges in your life and career.

You will find yourself spending less time anguishing and dreaming, and more time doing and accomplishing. What you once viewed as a big bet will soon seem so realistic that in the future you will think of it as a little bet.

Now take a moment to complete your next exercise before moving on to Lesson 4.

EXERCISE

Find an example in your life or job of a large upcoming goal that is very important for you to achieve. Think through the goal in detail and then use the following table to create your own think big, act small, move quick strategy, similar to the one in Table 3-1. Putting this on paper will make it more clear how you will be able to attain your big goal. If you reach a point at which you get hung up with a difficult decision, set a time frame for yourself to make the decision and then move on.

Think Big	Act Small	Move Quick

NOTES

BREAKING THROUGH PLATEAUS

Change is the law of life. And those who look only to the
past or present are certain to miss the future.

—JOHN F. KENNEDY

I n your life and career you should remain conscious of the
fact that the bend in the road does not have to be the end
of the road. As you seek to progress you will place yourself at
a point at which you can see past the bends in the road along
your journey and will be in a better position to successfully
manage your trajectory. If you do not position yourself this
way, you may have found your resting place, your plateau—
the point at which your trajectory is no longer continuing
upward in the traditional sense. As you will learn, the
acceptability of this is a matter of perspective based on where
you are currently in relation to your aspirations and goals.

It is at these plateau periods, which often are preceded by a period of success, when you will need to rapidly seek out new ideas and approaches. It is critically important to be aware of the possible dangers of a plateau in advance, as once you reach a plateau you will have lost considerable time and it will become harder to continue advancing at the same pace. In other words, you run the risk of experiencing a flat trajectory for a much longer period of time—or worse, becoming stagnant. Just as critically, others who have adapted and changed faster may already have solidified their position at the next step you had aimed for in your trajectory. In that case it will become even harder for you to break out of your plateau.

STAVING OFF A PLATEAU AT IBM

At some point along every continuum of success a plateau begins to appear. It is the natural evolution of any life cycle. When you accept that this will happen you will be better able to prepare for it. Thus, before reaching a plateau you must proactively plan for innovative and new ways of doing things. Without this, future growth becomes stalled. Consider IBM, which is one of the most successful and admired companies in the world. In 2012 IBM had revenue in excess of $104 billion and its profits approached $18 billion. But it wasn't always this way.

IBM was a dominant player in the computer server and PC space, but its fortunes began to change in the late 1980s. Part of the issue was that more than 90 percent of its profits came from its server business. IBM had become a one-trick pony and was not adequately prepared for a changing market. It had reached a plateau, which almost turned into a sustained failure. Consider this amount: $13.1 billion. That is how much money IBM lost in just two years!

Based on the many issues and risks facing the company, the IBM board of directors decided that changes were needed. What resulted was a change at the top and the surprise selection of Louis Gerstner Jr. as the new CEO. Not only was he an outsider to IBM, he also was not experienced in the technology sector. His appointment presented a daunting challenge, particularly because a number of analysts and many in the press vocally questioned his readiness or capability to fill the role.

One of the biggest problems Gerstner found at IBM was a culture of self-contentment and complacency. The attitude seemed to be that because IBM had been so successful in the past, it surely would remain that way. The company felt it could continue to ride a wave based on past success, when in reality the wave had washed ashore and IBM was left at a plateau. Even worse, it was a plateau that was beginning to turn downward toward stagnation. It would have been easy for Gerstner and his team to continue along the current path. Instead, Gerstner chose to do something different. He realized he had a choice: He could reach to break IBM out of the plateau, or continue to do much of the same and embark on a further downward spiral that might not stop.

He chose a bold course, which ultimately proved to transform the future of IBM. As Gerstner remarked, the actions the company would take would determine whether "IBM was merely going to be one more pleasant, safe, comfortable—but fairly innocuous—participant in the information technology industry, or whether we were once again going to be a company that mattered." In other words, he knew that IBM could remain on a possibly comfortable but irrelevant plateau, or do something drastically different and again become a leader in the field.

The first thing he did—and likely the most important—was to reverse course from the direction his predecessor had set. The prior CEO, John Akers, had secured support to break up IBM into multiple independent business units with the idea of enabling a structure that would allow decentralized market-driven decisions. Gerstner looked into the future and saw something different. He saw a market in which consumers wanted end-to-end solutions. He stated that he thought what consumers really wanted were comprehensive solutions with continued support. Working from that belief, he made a strategic decision to focus on which business units to keep and then to operate them as one company. He also bet big on the services sector, which grew exponentially to become a $30 billion part of IBM's business under his watch.

It is worth noting that Gerstner was well versed in the principles we reviewed in Lesson 1. As an outsider with a non-technology background, he knew that many answers and ideas would come from others. He spent considerable time seeking out opinions both inside and outside of IBM. He gathered feedback. The changes that Gerstner and IBM instituted were dramatic, but so were the subsequent accomplishments. Gerstner's actions were aligned with an old saying about wild ducks that the company had long used to express an important part of its culture. The idea behind it is that you can make wild ducks tame, but you cannot make tame ducks wild. In other words, once tamed, the ducks lose motivation and the desire to explore new things. Applied to work, it means that IBM realized it must give people room to do new and creative things. Not doing so would result in complacency and plateaus. As a testament to how much innovation has resulted from this philosophy, year-over-year IBM routinely receives more annual patents than does any other company.

INFLECTION POINTS

Along your career trajectory you will have moments at which you are approaching or are already at a critical juncture. Ideally it will be the former and you will notice it coming, which will provide you with more time to react and plan. Everybody has or will have one or more of these times during their career. Andy Grove from Intel, whose own critical moment we covered in Lesson 3, refers to these as *career inflection points*. It is very possible that had Grove made the wrong decision at his inflection point he would have had a much less illustrious career. In Figure 4-1 you can see that there are three different paths you can take leading out of a career inflection point. What's more, this will likely be a career-defining choice that you must make. Your decision

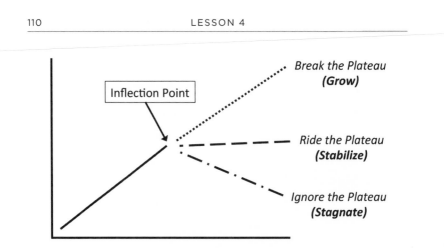

Figure 4-1: Career Inflection Point

can be distilled down to three options: you can decide to do something drastically different and break the plateau (grow), appreciate and ride the plateau (stabilize), or remain in denial and ignore the plateau (stagnate).

The top line represents what can happen if you embrace the opportunity and decide that it is time to enact radical change and do something that will set you apart. You use it as a time to grow. This growth could be in the form of self-improvement or developing new skills. It might involve searching for a new job, or perhaps even doing something entirely different.

The middle line indicates staying on the plateau. If this is the option you choose, you must go through a period of introspection and be clear on several points. First, if you continue doing what you are doing, will it be sustainable? Oftentimes it will not be and you could find yourself in the uncomfortable position of no longer adding value. If it will be sustainable, you then must decide whether you feel that you will remain content continuing to do what you are doing now. For some people, this will be just fine. However, because you are reading this book, it is unlikely that you will give serious consideration to any path other than growth.

It is essential during a plateau—a period of stabilization—to ensure that you do not let your trajectory begin to gradually point downward. When you become entrenched in one thing, you will over time lose the ability to innovate and progress. This will harm your trajectory. Life changes, markets change, and so too can your goals. It is up to you to chart your course, and that course can differ over time. Again, the important thing is to keep it from pointing down for too long.

In the next sections we will discuss the experiences of people who followed each of the first two paths shown in Figure 4-1, and reveal what happened as a result. The bottom line in the figure—the only line that points downward—is what happens when you remain in denial and refuse to accept the reality of a changed situation or choose to ignore it. In Lesson 5 we will cover this option, also known as stagnation, in more detail.

BREAK THE PLATEAU (GROW)

In 2008, at the age of fifty-nine, Joe Moglia announced his retirement as the CEO of TD Ameritrade after a very distinguished career. At that point he went on to do something radically different from what was expected for someone of his stature. When you trace Moglia's career trajectory it is easy to understand why so many people were shocked by what he did next.

By the young age of thirty-three, Moglia had established himself as the successful defensive coordinator of Dartmouth's football team—so successful that the team had won consecutive Ivy League titles the two prior seasons. And yet he had decided he was going to walk away. He seemingly gave up his dream of becoming the head coach of a Division I college football team and instead took an entry-level job at Merrill Lynch. Though it was not easy for him to leave coaching, he did so in order to be able to provide better financial footing for his family. He spent the next seventeen years at Merrill Lynch, and during that time rose through the ranks to a top executive role. When he left in 2001 it was to take the top post at TD Ameritrade. What followed under his leadership there was a remarkable turnaround of the then troubled company. In his seven years as CEO, TD Ameritrade grew from approximately $24 billion to $300 billion in assets managed—more than a twelve-fold increase!

When Moglia walked away from TD Ameritrade he embarked on a new path in his trajectory and showed amazing persistence along the way. His new path was actually back on his original trajectory. He had always dreamed of being the head coach of a Division I college football team and wanted to try again. To do so required financial sacrifice, and he went from being a CEO making millions of dollars a year to taking on a job as an unpaid "intern" with the University of Nebraska Cornhuskers. During his two years with the Cornhuskers he put in the same extreme hours as the paid coaches so that he could get back up to speed with the game he had left behind so long ago. He did so because he felt that this was the right strategic move in his trajectory and that it would lead toward a head coaching job at a Division I college. In 2011, at the age of 62, he took yet another step closer to that goal when he became a head coach for the first time with the Omaha Nighthawks of the United Football League (UFL).

After his one season in the UFL, Moglia applied for head coaching jobs at Division I schools. Finally he reached the point that he had always wanted in his trajectory; when he became the head coach of the Coastal Carolina University Chanticleers. Not only did he reach the target of his trajectory, he did something else: In his first year as coach the team won the conference championship and he was named the conference's coach of the year.

Moglia undoubtedly did not take the decision to leave TD Ameritrade lightly. It's hard enough to walk away from a job and career, let alone one that you are leading and in which you are financially secure. But he was at a good spot and likely saw that a plateau in his current role was approaching. It would be a place where he could do more, but his trajectory would not be as steep. Or as fulfilling.

Not everyone will need to go to the same extreme as Moglia to break out of a plateau, but it is important to be open to other opportunities and ways of doing things. One of the great things about your trajectory is that it is yours. Even if you go down one path, it is never too late to go down another. Perhaps no one exemplifies this better than Nola

Ochs, who at the age of ninety-five became the oldest person ever to receive a bachelor's degree. Not satisfied with stopping there, Ochs continued on and received her master's degree just three years later, in 2010. Changing course can be hard when everything is going well, but as Nola Ochs demonstrates, you can do it. Keep your eyes open and always be ready.

RIDE THE PLATEAU (STABILIZE)

Staying at a plateau does not have to be a bad thing. However, if you decide to remain at a plateau, you do need to accept and be content with your decision. What is critical for you to not only understand but to know about yourself is that your goals and aspirations will determine how you view a plateau. This is where positive and negative plateaus come into play. There could be times in your career when reaching a plateau is quite desirable. In fact, you may even reach a point at which a *permanent plateau* is desirable.

Consider Qiang, who was a successful lawyer at a Fortune 1000 company. Qiang had advanced rapidly up the hierarchy and had attained a senior-level position in the legal department at a relatively young age. Doing so required him to work long hours and travel excessively. Due to his success he was offered several more promotions, each of which he turned down. This befuddled his hard-charging bosses, who could not understand why this once promising attorney was no longer interested in greater impact, pay, and visibility.

I had worked with Qiang on several occasions, and when I asked him about this he stated that it was quite simple. He

had sacrificed a great deal early in his career while he sought
to advance and reach the role he had always desired. Once he
did he found that he was no longer interested in continuing to
advance upward in the organization. He had reached a
position where he really enjoyed what he was doing with the
specialty area of law that he was practicing. What he realized
is that he was comfortable with reaching what became a permanent plateau.

Because Qiang decided that a permanent plateau was acceptable, this became a *positive plateau* in his mind. Instead
of this being a negative, he found it appealing and fulfilling.
Had he wanted to advance further but been unable to do so,
he would have instead experienced a *negative plateau*. With
a negative plateau you will not find comfort or satisfaction.
You will instead feel that you are stifled and no longer progressing.

Or consider Claudia, who after several promotions had
become a general manager. After about a year in this role, she
was approached about a new assignment leading the opening
of a new location, with the opportunity to then progress into
a market-based role with responsibility for multiple locations.
While Claudia was grateful for the support and recognition,
she indicated that she was not interested in changing jobs.
Like Qiang's, her reasons were rather simple. In addition to
being fulfilled in her role, she knew that her family had really
grown attached to the area where they were living and their
local community. She did not want to have to face multiple
moves that would require uprooting her family and the ties
they had established. Claudia really liked her team and made

an internal commitment that her goal would be to continue to grow and to make her location the best and most successful in the company. It's hard to have an issue with that type of attitude and commitment. Claudia is another example of someone who found her own positive plateau.

I want to be clear that a positive plateau does not mean that you can rest on your laurels. You still will need to evolve and keep up with the change of pace for your role. Being comfortable at a plateau does not suggest that you can stop developing, learning, or performing. If you let that happen, what was once a positive plateau will quickly turn negative.

STABILIZATION AND FLOW

Since a plateau can be desirable at some points in your career, we should also recognize key career benefits that can be garnered during this time. A plateau can afford you a time of stability and an opportunity for deep learning. This stable period may even seem like a resting point in your career, because you are well-versed enough with what you are doing that it seems like you are putting in less effort than you had to in the past. However, in almost all situations achieving this level of competence does not mean that you have fully mastered something. There is always more to learn.

It is important for you to realize that you are approaching or are at a plateau, and then decide what you want to do about it. Like Qiang and Claudia, you may reach a point at which you very much enjoy what you are doing and want to continue doing that for the indefinite future. There is nothing wrong with this. However, if you want to move on to something different or bigger you will need to quickly chart a course away from the plateau. If you spend too much time on a plateau you will move from a period of stability to a time of stagnation, which occurs when you lose ground against others in relation to your planned trajectory. As you will learn in Lesson 5, this can be caused by several factors, including not building new skills, not innovating, or becoming complacent.

Realizing the importance of not becoming complacent, a positive aspect of spending a stabilizing period of time in a plateau is that it can afford you the opportunity to reach a state of mastery over a given area. In what Mihály Csíkszentmihályi calls *flow*, you become so proficient at something that you reach a point at which you feel complete mastery over what you are doing and develop a strong sense of control and self-confidence. Something that was once difficult for you may seem to become effortless. Or you may be so stimulated by an activity—even if you have not mastered it—that you lose track of time.

Have you ever found yourself in just such a state of concentration and engagement with an activity at work? Has this happened to the point that you lost track of the time? Perhaps it resulted in your missing lunch, or being late for a meeting. If so, you likely were in a state of flow. And it is also likely that you were engaged in an activity that met three primary conditions: you enjoyed it, it required concentration, and you had the capability to do it.

The conditions for flow are maximized when a task is not simple and when a person has considerable skill and interest in the activity. Csíkszentmihályi uses the example of surgeons as having a job that's prime for flow. Not only do successful surgeons have great passion in their job, but the conditions required to start flow (high level of concentration, no distractions in operating room, etc.) are optimal. In an experiment in which he monitored how often workers experienced flow, Csíkszentmihályi found that higher frequency of flow was associated with higher satisfaction on the job. If you never experience flow at work and are constantly watching the clock and waiting to go home, you have not found a job you enjoy. This is an indicator that you need to begin looking for a new step in your trajectory.

Flow does not occur when you are disengaged in an activity, nor when you lack the skill to do it. Skill in any activity is something that can be developed and mastered over time, but you must have the baseline capability for it. It requires excessive practice. However, it cannot be just any type of practice; it must be deliberate and focused. If you want to learn to play the piano, practice will be much more powerful if you turn off the television and remove yourself from all distractions. It will be even better if you have clear goals and a plan for practice that you follow. Add to that getting immediate feedback on your performance, and your practice will have even more positive effects.

Research by K. Anders Ericsson and colleagues has shown that to truly master an activity a minimum of ten years of focused practice is needed. This has been popularized as the 10,000-hour rule, which is based on the approximate amount of practice that experts in a given field put in during those ten years that separates them from others. At work, if you are constantly moving from one role to another, you are learning rapidly but are not affording yourself the time for deep learning. A plateau can provide you with a time to conduct this deliberate practice. Of course, by the time you are at a plateau you will have spent much time learning already. Consequently you have likely amassed years of "practice" in your area of expertise. Ericsson goes back to research from 1897 by William Bryan and Noble Harter, who recognized this when looking at plateaus in the skill acquisition capabilities of Morse code operators. The researchers found that when the operators were at a plateau (i.e., their skills were no longer improving naturally), the plateau could be broken by putting those workers through deliberate and focused training.

If you recall persistence and intrinsic motivation from Lesson 2, you will realize that these are two of the key factors that can result in reaching a state of flow at work. It is hard to put in deliberate practice without persistence, and it is equally difficult to persist if you are not motivated in your area of work. When you have these two qualities, though, you will be able to increase your skills to find that state of flow. You could even begin to feel like you have the "Midas Touch" and that everything you do will seemingly turn to gold.

Finally, during a period of stabilization you can build up the skills to not only improve in your current role, but to prepare for your next one. In many ways you are expanding the skills that will make your transition to the next step easier.

This will leave you with more energy and optimism as you approach your next challenge.

LOOK PAST SUCCESS TO NEW INNOVATION

It is important to not fixate only on that which has made you successful. While you do not want to forget your successes, dwelling on them for too long can become problematic. Doing so will close your eyes to transcendent trends that could turn into permanent game changers. If you catch these early you may be able to propel yourself forward. Missing them, however, could lead to a downward trajectory and prevent you from developing new or innovative skills, approaches, or products on your own. When you focus only on your success, it becomes easy to miss what is happening around you. Then, once you do realize what is happening, you will already be at a plateau.

Consider the news on June 29, 2012, when CNN and *Forbes* ran very different, yet inextricably related stories. *Forbes* was covering a major milestone in the life of Apple; CNN was reviewing how far a once booming company had fallen in recent years. *Forbes* was covering the five-year anniversary of the iPhone and celebrating its tremendous success, whereas CNN was discussing the amazing decline of RIM, the maker of the once omnipotent BlackBerry phone.

The success of the iPhone was directly related to the near-complete collapse of RIM. The main differentiator? Innovation. Steve Jobs and Apple never stopped innovating. RIM, however, could never get past the success of the BlackBerry.

Though that phone was once an amazing device—and had a nearly complete hold on the important corporate market— RIM was late to the game in adapting. It did not see what was happening around it in the market and so did not make the necessary course corrections. It had become complacent based on its past success and drifted quickly into a plateau. Any changes it did make were minor and did not substantively break the mold from the products it had made in the past. Conversely, Apple continued to release new products and enjoyed a steady rise because of its continual innovation of products.

A. G. Lafley once stated, "The best way to win in this world is through innovation." As the CEO of Procter & Gamble he realized the importance of this and refers to innovation as the *game changer*. He notes, however, that innovation by itself is not sufficient. You also need to execute against your goals and priorities. Without doing so, innovation can be rendered nearly meaningless. Even all of the innovation by Apple would be to no avail if the company could not also build and deliver the products on time.

Like Lafley and so many others, you should consider innovation as one of the most important devices you have at your disposal to get past a plateau. You must constantly be looking for ways to innovate and seek out novel solutions both to problems and opportunities. Keep in mind that novel does not need to mean difficult solutions. Nor does innovate need to mean new. That is one of the great things about so many innovative solutions: more times than not you already have the answer. You just need to release your mental holds and identify what is often right in front of you. The smart-phone was not invented by Apple; there were many models already in the market when the company released the iPhone. Apple simply innovated by taking something already in existence and creating an intuitive design with features and capabilities that surpassed anything else available.

In his classic book *On Problem Solving*, the late German psychologist Karl Duncker described a series of experiments he conducted to assess barriers that keep people from finding the right solution to a given problem. For example, participants were given six matchsticks and asked to find a way to create four equilateral triangles. Blinded by standard ways of thinking, few participants could find the correct solution, which is actually rather straightforward. Go ahead and see if you can figure this out. If you are stuck, see the solution on page 126.

In a much more commonly referenced problem, Duncker gave people three small boxes: one with matches, one with three candles, and a third filled with tacks (the experiments used multiple variations, including giving the matches and candles without a box, and filling the boxes with material—such as buttons—that were irrelevant to the solution). The instructions were quite simple—participants were asked to find a way to affix the candles to the wall and to ensure that no wax would drip onto the floor once lit. This is an example of a situation in which the answer was right in front of them, yet many failed to see it. They saw the boxes as holders of the various pieces of the puzzle, but not as part of it.

In fact, the best solution is to empty the boxes and then affix each to the wall with tacks, with the opening of the box facing upward. After doing so the candles could be placed in the boxes and lit. People in the experiment were confined by what Duncker termed *functional fixedness*. More simply put, it was constrained thinking that prevented people from solving the problem. When this occurs, you see something only for what it is, and miss seeing what it could be. In this case, many participants saw a matchbox, a tack box, and a box of candles, and failed to see that the boxes could actually be repurposed as candleholders.

On an organizational level, W. Chan Kim and Renee Mauborgne explored innovation through evaluating companies that pursued what the authors termed a *red ocean* or *blue ocean* strategy. With a red ocean approach you are trying to compete in an existing area, one where the competition is known. In contrast, with a blue ocean approach you are diving into unknown areas where the market space is not known. While it is important to be aware of the red oceans, by charting into blue oceans you can really innovate and differentiate yourself.

In many ways a red ocean approach is defensive, whereas a blue ocean strategy is proactive. The reason for terming this scenario *red ocean* is that the waters become bloody because of the cutthroat nature of those who are competing against you. By moving into blue oceans you can focus more on yourself and what you feel you need to do in order to innovate and succeed. You consequently create an internal competition, which results in a more fulfilling and positive outcome that does not involve cutting others down.

BE A BEST PRACTICE

Organizations are constantly searching for best practices they can adopt to gain an edge. Doing this too much, however, can create a problem. A best practice is learned from those who are already ahead. You are just playing catch-up. By simply adopting a best practice you can only get yourself to a point of parity. To really excel you need to refine and create best practices. When you do so you can utilize these skills before the best practice has become a common practice. You want your brand and skills to be at a point where others seek you out to learn from you. When you reach that level you can serve as a mentor to help others, which as you learned in Lesson 1 can be of great value. When you are not able to stay ahead in this manner you increase your risk of stalling at a plateau.

When Henry Ford forever changed the way we travel, he was thinking ahead. Sam Walton did the same when he realized that he could shave costs through building and managing the best logistics network in the world. Steve Jobs did it when he revolutionized the tablet computer. Bill Walsh did it when his West Coast Offense transformed the passing game in professional football. Each of these individuals looked for opportunities and capitalized on them, creating best practices that were emulated by other people and organizations. To do the same in your career you must be willing and able to put in the effort to change faster than others. Consider the fact that it is much harder to notice yourself aging than it is to notice how much a friend whom you have not seen in a long time has aged. That is because it is harder to see what is slowly changing in front of you. Now place this against the context of your workplace. If that is all you know and pay attention to, you may not notice how quickly things outside of it are changing.

CONCLUSION

What is unique about plateaus is that your individual circumstances determine how you should view one at any given time. Plateaus are not always bad, nor are they always good. A plateau is situational. What may be a negative plateau to one person is a positive plateau or ideal state for another. Qiang and Claudia were talented employees with great capabilities and chances for further upward promotion, but for their own reasons each decided to turn down desirable career opportunities. The primary reason was that they both truly enjoyed what they were doing.

When you do take a step forward in your trajectory, do not allow yourself to bask in the moment for too long. The skills that got you there are not always the skills that will keep you there. If you rest, you will plateau. In sports we often hear of athletes whose production falls after they receive a big contract. They just spent several years building a successful track record of performance to warrant the new contract. All too often they bask in that success and do not continue to reach for greater things. They may continue to perform well, but they never take it to the next level—the level that was expected of them.

Plateaus may provide a point of reflection. Maybe it is time for you to consider moving toward something else. You may want to explore a new trajectory that perhaps you had not thought of before or, as Moglia did, reconsider a once desired trajectory that you had given up on or left long ago. If you are reading this and are frustrated with where you are now, consider whether it is where you thought you would be and if it is what you want to be doing. If not, was there something else that you were once passionate about to which you could return?

Ultimately you must decide which path to take if you reach a plateau. It will probably be one of the two discussed in this lesson. The right choice will be the one that provides you with the most enjoyment and fulfillment at work and in life.

On the next page is another exercise for you to complete before we turn to Lesson 5, which covers the third option coming out of a plateau: stagnation.

Solution to Karl Duncker's puzzle: In order to create four equilateral triangles you must create a three-dimensional figure with the matchsticks. Most people do not change their thinking and continue to try two-dimensional approaches to solve this problem.

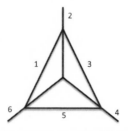

Figure reprinted with permission of APA from Karl Duncker, "On Problem Solving," trans. Lynne S. Lees, *Psychological Monographs* 58:26 (1945), published by APA.

EXERCISE

Each of the following two columns contains ten words. Take a moment to consider how you most often feel about your current job and where you are in your career. Circle the words in each column that describe how you frequently feel.

Stuck	Happy
Limited	Fulfilled
Bored	Excited
Demotivated	Engaged
Angry	Challenged
Stretched	Motivated
Burned out	Eager
Frustrated	Relevant
Meaningless	Enthusiastic
Discouraged	Meaningful

Now count up the total number of circles in each column. If you have one or two more circles in the first column than in the second you are likely approaching a plateau. If you have many more circles in the first column than you do in the second, you are likely at a negative plateau and you need to take quick action to break out of it. If you have more circles in the second column, you are at a good place and are not at an immediate risk for a negative plateau.

NOTES

LESSON 5

AVOIDING THE STAGNATION TRAP

That some achieve great success, is proof to all

that others can achieve it as well.

—ABRAHAM LINCOLN

The thirty companies that make up the Dow Jones Industrial Average (DJIA) are often thought of as the gold standard when it comes to top organizations. They are chosen based on their past performance and success. These are the blue-chip companies that set the standard of excellence for others. Despite this, you might be surprised to learn that the DJIA is notoriously fickle when it comes to stability. Instead of remaining constant, the companies included in it change quite frequently. In fact, the companies in the DJIA have changed forty-eight times since its founding in 1896; only General Electric remains as an original member. As of 2012, less than half of the companies (thirteen to be exact) had been added before 1990. Another way to put this into perspective is that more than half of the organizations were replaced in the past twenty years.

If these organizations have had such successful performance track records, why is it that this group of great companies changes so much? Even massive companies such as General Motors and Citigroup—leaders in their industries— declined and were removed from the DJIA. This often happens because these companies stagnate and fail to maintain the significant advantage they previously held over their competition. They typically lose that edge—and sometimes fail entirely—because the leadership did not adapt to changing conditions and chart a proper trajectory to avoid what we call stagnation. Instead of constantly searching for ways to stay ahead of the curve, these companies lost their way. It is easy for the DJIA to maintain stability and avoid stagnation because underperforming companies can be replaced with better-performing companies, thereby maintaining more apparent stability.

Unlike the DJIA, you do not have a similar ability to almost instantaneously swap something out if it is no longer working. If your house loses value, for example, you cannot maintain your equity by exchanging it for a house whose value is equivalent to your original purchase price. The same principle applies in your career. It is therefore essential that you continually map out your own trajectory so you will not lose the progress or career capital you have gained. You will need to avoid complacency in order to avoid decline. You must create and maintain your own premium at work. The consequence of not doing so is that your organization could "swap" you for a better-performing employee. You will be able to prevent this outcome by ensuring that you never become stagnant.

This is particularly relevant when you consider that in many high-growth industries and companies the requirements of your job can quickly overtake your current skills. More specifically, a change in job performance expectations can easily outpace the speed of your own skill development if you are not careful. This will require you to constantly expand your skills and identify ways to improve. Without this continual growth, and at times reinvention, you run the risk of stagnation, which is counter to the positive concepts we have covered.

A key element in avoiding stagnation is to be aware of what you need to change in order to stay ahead. If you are not careful, your past success can easily become your biggest impediment to sustained success. In addition to not letting your past success prevent your continued change and growth, you must break unproductive habits and reinvest that energy into productive pursuits. The extra energy you exert to expand your skills will pay great dividends and enable you to remain ahead.

STAGNATION IN CONCEPT

Stagnation can be defined as a failure to develop, progress, or advance, which has the effect of leading you down a negative trajectory. When you stagnate you are in a state of decline.

The decline can be gradual or abrupt and can be viewed either in comparison to others or to the trajectory you were once on. Unfortunately, when this process occurs gradually the changes can be subtle and hard to notice until you are long down the path. When you place this concept in the context of your career it has enormous implications. Rarely, though, is there even an awareness or discussion of stagnation in the workplace.

Sometimes the decline is of your own doing. Maybe you did not get the promotion you wanted; maybe you no longer enjoy your job; maybe there was another reason. Other times it has to do with the pace at which you are learning and adapting compared to others. What often happens is that your skills are not keeping up with changing conditions, and others are moving forward while you are moving downward in comparison. This is a very important point for you to consider. You can do exactly the same thing that you have always done successfully and still stagnate. It happens because others are progressing and building their skills at a faster rate than you are, which in the end means you are actually losing ground.

Stagnation is sometimes confused with being at a plateau. However, as we discussed in Lesson 4, plateaus are not necessarily always negative. This fact is the key difference between stagnating and reaching a plateau. Unlike a plateau, stagnation will always have negative consequences because it results in a deterioration of your skills, either directly or indirectly. When your skills deteriorate you provide others with a prime opportunity to overtake you. At times this can be very hard to notice because you can be somewhat sheltered at work. In other words, your most immediate comparison is to those around you.

In order to avoid stagnation you also need to keep pace with changes in the environment and the competitive landscape beyond your job. As discussed in Lesson 1, oftentimes people are so focused on the duties of their job that they forget to look around to see what is changing now or might soon be. Though these changes may not seem important today, they could quickly become very relevant to your continued success. To help avoid stagnation remember to take into account all of the rings in your feedback knowledge circle (Figure 1-1). Input from each of those areas is valuable for keeping up with what is happening around you.

It is essential for you to realize that avoiding stagnation is directly under your control. This actually applies to individuals, teams, organizations, and even entire economies. Indeed, Zanny Minton Beddoes wrote in the *Economist* that 2012 could be the year of self-induced economic stagnation. She relates economic policy problems—particularly in Europe—to a series of preventable reasons. Beddoes argues that even in cases in which leaders know what should be done, they continually avoid making important changes in order to avoid the possibility of undermining others' confidence. She lays out reasons why the global recession will last longer than necessary because of *avoidable errors*.

Avoidable errors are just that—avoidable. Avoidable does not mean that it will be easy, but it does mean that you can prevent it. An avoidable error can take the form of an unnecessary mistake, delaying or failing to make a decision, neglecting to learn from the past, or not adapting to a changing environment. Consider this against the economic stagnation that Beddoes writes about. Governments are not moving quickly enough, nor are they addressing the problems with the right magnitude and fortitude. Rather than making the larger changes that are necessary, Beddoes says, leaders continue to take the safe but ineffective middle road with their proposed solutions. Use this as an example of what not to do in your effort to prevent or move past stagnation. Sometimes little tweaks will be sufficient, but many times you will need to make big changes in order to stay ahead. Do not be afraid to take calculated risks in this regard. As is true with the economy, you may be able to plug along with safety, but eventually it will catch up with you.

TYPES OF STAGNATION

There are two types of stagnation you need to be aware of and elude. The first is known as *intrapersonal stagnation*, and the second as *interpersonal stagnation*. While both can be dangerous to your career, you particularly need to be careful to avoid intrapersonal stagnation. If you ever feel that you are stalled in your career, or that things are not moving fast enough, you should quickly attempt to determine whether one of these types of stagnation is the reason.

The state of intrapersonal stagnation is self-induced and will result in your proceeding on a negative trajectory for a period of time. It often begins to take hold at stages during

your career when self-doubt creeps in. This could happen because you are uncertain about a particular job or project. It
also occurs when you spend too much time reevaluating what
you are doing and become mired in uncertainty over which
direction to take next. You become entrenched due to that
uncertainty, and your excitement and interest in your work
then begins to decline. If you are not fully vested in what you
are doing it becomes all too easy to fall into a rut and let your
performance suffer. This is intrapersonal stagnation. It is
driven by events that are fully under your control, and is not
directly impacted by external events or conditions.

When you consider intrapersonal stagnation in the context of your trajectory, you can see that it will always lead in
a downward direction. Figure 5-1 illustrates what occurs
when intrapersonal stagnation develops. You have a desired
trajectory, and then you allow an event or events to derail it.
This could be brought on by an internal situation or by
external events such as an industry downturn and the fear of
layoffs. The solid line represents your desired long-term trajectory; the top dotted line represents how you were trending
before the event; and the bottom dotted line shows what
actually happened after the derailing event. What you can see
is a large gap—or opportunity loss—from where you were
trending with your trajectory to where you actually are. What
this underscores is that your opportunity loss is not the difference from the point at which your stagnation began. No,
it is actually the difference between where you are now and
where you would have been had you not allowed yourself to
become derailed.

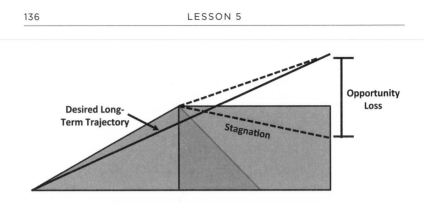

Figure 5-1: Intrapersonal Stagnation

Alyssa, who worked for a large international conglomerate, succumbed to intrapersonal stagnation. She believed she had a product proposal that would generate millions of dollars in incremental sales and spent a great deal of time studying the market and developing a strong business case. Her approach was meticulously detailed, and there was very little to pick apart. She had supporting market research and focus group data from existing and possible future customers. The financials looked strong. When Alyssa shared the proposal with the business development management team she received a good response and was asked to come back with some additional information in one month. She left feeling very confident that her idea would be approved after the next meeting.

When Alyssa returned with the follow-up proposal she was stunned that the response she received was much less enthusiastic than the first one had been. In fact, what she encountered was more like resistance. Even though she had what she thought was a bulletproof proposal, it was rejected during the actual meeting and she was asked to no longer pursue it. Alyssa felt misled and could not understand why this happened. She started to develop her own "story" about what had happened, and quickly began to feel that management was out to get her and wanted her to fail. Consequently, her once positive attitude started to turn negative. During this time her work performance suffered and others began to try to avoid her at the office. She started looking for a new job and left the company just a few months later.

What Alyssa did not account for in her story was that during the month after her initial presentation a large product recall and negative publicity had impacted one of the company's key products, which was in the same product category as her proposal. She viewed the rejection of her proposal as management not listening to her ideas or not appreciating her contribution. It was just the opposite. Management really did like her proposal, but the timing was no longer right for it. They liked it enough that her suggestion was fully adopted shortly after she left the company and was well received in the marketplace. As Alyssa projected, it did in fact generate the expected amount of incremental income for the company.

Though the product took off well, Alyssa's personal trajectory stagnated when she left. The job she took was very similar to her previous job, and instead of developing new skills most of her time was spent learning the new company, building relationships, and reestablishing herself. As a result, her trajectory unnecessarily went down for a period of time.

In the context of Figure 5-1, she could have maintained the top line, but she let an event lead her to stagnate and start down the path in the lower dotted line. Had Alyssa taken time to more fully understand the dynamics surrounding her proposal she may have avoided stagnation. Her mistake was similar to the one Jan made when she went through her company's promotional process (Lesson 1). If Alyssa had simply asked anyone a clarifying question about why her proposal was not adopted, she might have quickly found out that it was not because of something she had done wrong.

Though it is not as damaging to your career as intrapersonal stagnation, interpersonal stagnation is also something you need to be aware of and try to prevent. If intrapersonal stagnation is about independently allowing yourself to lapse, interpersonal stagnation is about allowing yourself to fall short compared to those around you. It occurs when *external* conditions and competition change more rapidly than you do.

Figure 5-2 shows the consequences of interpersonal stagnation. Let's say that you and a peer are in the same job and are generally equivalent performers. Then a market advancement or organizational change that requires a modification or innovation of skills comes along. You, on the one hand, do not sufficiently notice this need and keep doing the same thing that has worked for you in the past. Your peer, on the other hand, realizes that conditions have changed and quickly adjusts. Even though your own general performance trajectory is the same, it in effect has diminished because of the changed conditions. The trajectory of your peer, represented

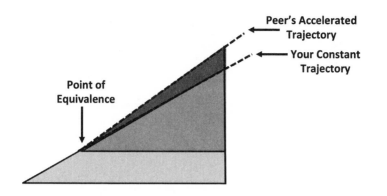

Figure 5-2: Interpersonal Stagnation

by the upper dotted line, can be compared to yours in the lower line. The gap between the two shows how you have now stagnated in comparison. In other words, you are still doing well, as illustrated by your positive trajectory, but you lost your point of equivalence and are now trending lower than your peer.

Interpersonal stagnation can occur at both an individual and organizational level. Consider Netflix and its impact on Blockbuster. Almost since its inception Netflix has been a darling to investors and welcomed by audiences at home who wanted to watch movies in a convenient way. Netflix was conceived in part because its cofounder, Reed Hastings, had a disdain for the late fees charged by traditional brick-and-mortar movie rental chains such as Blockbuster. What started as a movie delivery service for DVDs has continued to evolve in order to keep pace with—and even drive—changes in technology and consumer needs. Netflix could have maintained a strong plateau and remained the market leader in DVD delivery service, but the company realized that to stay ahead it would need to constantly adapt and change.

One of the major shifts the company made was to expand its number of offerings, and to also include the option to download various televisions shows in addition to movies. Early on Netflix recognized the changing technology landscape and expanded its service offerings to include the ability for people to download and stream movies from their home computers, and then even from mobile devices. More recently Netflix moved into creating its own entertainment content, starting with the acclaimed series *House of Cards*.

Hastings has been incredibly adept at finding opportunities where others did not realize a need existed. He was finding blue oceans (Lesson 4). Perhaps more important, he has not become complacent with any of the Netflix successes. He continually has probed and done research to find ways to improve and further expand his business. In *Demand: Creating What People Love Before They Know They Want It*, Adrian Slywotzky reviews the rather ominous start to Netflix, when subscriber growth was anemic. Only San Francisco—the site of Netflix headquarters and its distribution center—had a decent subscription rate. Hastings and his team needed to know why, so they collected subscriber data to understand differences across customer bases. What they found was that subscribers in San Francisco loved Netflix because they received their DVDs so quickly due to the proximity of the distribution center (DC). Based on the results of the data

Netflix began to open more DCs and found that subscriber rates in the areas near those centers soon jumped.

Compare this to Blockbuster, which was the preeminent movie rental company in the United States. Instead of recognizing and going after the opportunity in this new area of online content, the company simply stayed its course, rested for a while at a plateau, and then fell quickly into stagnation. What might have been a relatively modest investment if done sooner instead became a massive effort by Blockbuster to catch up to Netflix. Ultimately the effort failed. By the time Blockbuster tried to gain a foothold in this emerging market space it was so far behind that the company had to file for bankruptcy.

In *The Innovator's Dilemma*, Clayton Christensen explores this type of problem at the organizational level through his insightful analysis of why many successful companies fail. He states that these companies are doing the right things, but they paradoxically fail for just that reason. They fail for doing more of what made them great in the first place. Meanwhile, other companies are moving past that point and taking advantage of new approaches, enabling them to jump ahead of the competition. Companies that fail in this manner serve as examples of interpersonal stagnation. One of the case studies Christensen provides involves the manufacturers of the original floppy disk drives. There was a market leader for 14-inch disks, then 8-inch, then 5-inch, and then 3.5-inch. However, the market leaders were not the same across these size categories. Each time, it was a competitor that came in to take over the next evolution.

The reason each of these manufacturers lost its advantage was because it focused too much on improving its current product, and not enough on moving to the next big one. Ironically, the market leader of the new technology often had developed but failed to implement the next-generation disk. So while Memorex actually led the charge for designing 8-inch disks, it was Seagate Technology that pioneered that market. Memorex had a split loyalty between the successful 14-inch drive and the new—and at that time only potentially successful—8-inch disks. As a result, Memorex spent more time investing in the 14-inch drives and less on moving to the next big thing, in this case the smaller 8-inch disk.

This same concept applies to your career. Do not allow something in which you have had considerable success prevent you from finding your next big thing. Others will be quick to realize that change is needed and will accelerate away from you if you do not do so first. Consider a point made by Malcolm Gladwell in his book *The Tipping Point*, in which he uses diffusion research to explain how new products are brought into and become successful in the market. When something is introduced into the market, not everyone purchases it at the same time. For example, when televisions first appeared some people ran out to buy one, while others waited decades to purchase one (or perhaps never did). When exploring diffusion in terms of the way innovations and products are adopted, it becomes clear that two of the most critical roles are filled by those individuals in the groups known as Innovators and Mavens. These are the people who see a movement and embrace it before everyone else. They are the early adopters of products and technology. Similarly, they are also the early identifiers and adopters of new skills.

In your career you should aspire to be an Innovator or Maven in your pursuit to be among the first to find critical new skills that you must develop. Doing so will provide you with a great differentiator at work. If you wait longer you will become a member of one of the other groups described by Gladwell (Early Majority, Late Majority, and Laggards), at which point you will simply be playing catch-up with the leaders. Typically each group serves as a reference point for the subsequent groups to watch and learn from. When you are an Innovator in acquiring new skills to attain greater success at work, other people will watch and learn from you. And because they are learning *from you* it means you will keep an advantage in maintaining your trajectory.

A $100-BILLION LOSS

If we return for a moment to the DJIA, a further analysis of the companies that have been removed or added to the index will show you just how quickly a trajectory can change. As an example, let's take a quick look at Eastman Kodak. Eastman Kodak was added to the DJIA in 1930 and remained as part of the index for seventy-four years. In 2004 it was dropped and replaced by American Insurance Group (AIG). Eastman Kodak, of course, was one of the world's most recognizable brands, but still lost its way and had to be substituted. Fast-forward and AIG also lost its edge. Just four years after AIG was added it was replaced by Kraft Foods! Think about this. AIG was viewed by experts as such a strong company that it was chosen to replace Eastman Kodak and yet only four years later it was removed.

The decision to drop a company is not taken lightly, nor is the selection of the new company. That is why it is amazing to watch how quickly fortunes can change if you are not careful. When it was added to the DJIA in 2004 AIG had stated a net income of over $11 billion (this was later revised downward by over $1 billion). When it was removed in 2008 losses of nearly $100 billion were reported, a difference of $110 *billion* from 2004! AIG had made some very bad investment decisions that resulted in a negative financial impact to many people. Ultimately AIG was given a second chance to survive thanks to a government bailout to the tune of $182 billion. Fast-forward to 2011, and AIG reported a profit of $16 billion. AIG was eventually able to recover through a series of prudent decisions, including refocusing on its core insurance business. The company was willing to ask for and accept help and, critically, learn from its mistakes and admit where it was wrong.

From the mistakes of AIG you can pull important lessons for your own career. While recovery from mistakes is possible, you may have a long road to climb back depending on the egregiousness of the error. AIG managed to quickly find financial recovery, but even now has not fully reclaimed the positive reputation it once had. AIG thought it was wisely making money from a series of derivative contracts that were tied to mortgages. However, once the housing market burst AIG no longer had the liquidity necessary to cover payment to creditors. One such major mistake can result in an unwinding. Be careful that you do not become so blindly confident in yourself that you play it too loose and make grave errors. You should remain confident, but do not act like AIG and use your confidence and past success to create the false assumption that you are incapable of making a mistake.

If you react quickly and swiftly you can undo major mistakes before stagnation takes over. I think of Jessica, who was not performing very well in her job. Her supervisor knew that she had greater potential and had a conversation with her about how she could improve her performance. When she still did not improve she was placed on a performance improvement plan (PIP). With a PIP an employee is usually given a certain amount of time to improve performance. If there is no improvement more severe consequences can occur, including termination.

When she received the PIP Jessica had an eye-opening moment. It was at this point that she realized her trajectory was at risk and that she must take immediate steps to improve. Over the next few months Jessica focused intensely on the improvement needs outlined in the PIP. She refreshed and expanded her knowledge in areas critical to her job and began to perform better using this new knowledge. Ultimately she was taken off of the PIP thanks to her improved performance. Jessica's story gets even better. Just a little more than a year later, she was actually promoted and took on a new job with greater responsibility. Jessica's example underscores the importance of acting before it is too late. Had she waited any longer to adjust she likely would have fully stagnated and potentially even lost her job.

Finally, seeking help is usually wise and is not construed as a sign of weakness. You will not need to seek a massive financial bailout like AIG, but you can look to others for advice and guidance. When you reach out for development you put yourself in a position to be able to advance in areas in which you could otherwise become stagnant. As you have already learned, this is increasingly important in the modern workforce, where skills become stagnant faster than ever because of rapidly changing technological advancements.

Conditions and skills necessary to succeed are changing faster now than at any point in modern human history. How many times have you heard people talk about "the good old days" with fondness? How many times have you talked about them yourself? The good old days are normally in reference to a time several decades ago, a time that was easier. But the world changes much quicker now. In fact, the good old days might be only five years ago, or even less. We talk of a time before cell phones. We can't imagine life without the Internet. Or without Google. Or GPS in our cars. The world is now evolving so quickly that you must be an expert at adaptation and reinvention. You must be able to change what you do and how you do it. This does not imply that you need to change who you are. Instead, you must change your skill sets and think ahead. If you do not adapt quickly you will become stagnant or, worse, irrelevant. Not adapting quickly is particularly dangerous in both large and fast-moving companies. In those types of situations others will view you as an obstacle to progress and will begin to find ways to work around you instead of with you.

I am reminded of a colleague who saw industry changes happening and took extra initiative to avoid stagnation. Bill had been on an analytics team for more than ten years and was considered the go-to person when it came to handling large sets of data. He knew all of the shortcuts in Microsoft Excel and was able to work with the data more quickly than were his peers. The amount of data his organization collected was increasing exponentially, and Bill realized he would no longer be able to keep up with the data needs of the company using his old approach with Excel. Bill knew that he needed to expand his skill set so that he could better manage the "Big Data" that corporations are scrambling to manage and better understand. In doing so he exhibited the characteristics of a Maven.

As soon as he recognized this need, Bill reached out to his boss to express his interest in learning more about this area. His boss realized how this could be beneficial and agreed to send Bill to an upcoming conference on the topic, and also to fund tuition for a night class on analytics. Not only did this enable Bill to learn more to avoid stagnating, but he also was considerably more engaged in his job because of his excitement with the topic and the support that his boss provided. Moreover, he was able to quickly apply his new education to the job and further increase his contribution to the organization. Bill is a wonderful example of how not to drift into stagnation.

He recognized an opportunity and reacted quickly. Had he waited it would have been more difficult and time consuming for him to catch up and acquire the new skills.

HALTING STAGNATION

Stagnation can occur at any point in your career or life. Stagnation can take the form of being risk averse, and it often begins with a setback. Other times it occurs as a result of not paying attention to what is in front of you, to what others are doing. This is not insurmountable, and the true measure is how you react to the setback.

The Olympic gold medalist and National Hockey League Hall of Famer Mario Lemieux—who played for the Pittsburgh Penguins—is a great example. During his career he had problems with his back, which resulted in his missing more than 100 games during the first nine years of his career. But then he was dealt an even bigger career setback when he was diagnosed with cancer early in 1993. A month later he began a series of twenty-two radiation treatments. What is truly amazing is what he did right after his final treatment: He not only boarded a plane to rejoin the team but also actually played in the game that night. While many were surprised, others felt that this was Lemieux's plan all along. He had prepared every day during his treatment with the intent to return as quickly as possible. As Lemieux stated, during his radiation treatments he was always thinking positively about not just returning to the NHL but also regaining the NHL scoring title. This strong self-confidence enabled him to think ahead and to avoid the negativity and doubt that can all too easily turn into stagnation.

Lemieux provides us with an incredible illustration of choosing one's own trajectory. When diagnosed with cancer, he did not stagnate and let his trajectory point down. He could have used his illness as a reason to stop training. He already was one of the most accomplished players in league history, and no one would have questioned him had he decided to retire. Everyone would have understood. But no, Lemieux decided that he was going to push past the cancer. Not only did he do that, he again became the NHL scoring champion, just as he told himself he would when he was diagnosed.

One of the hardest things you need to do to avoid stagnation is to change your approach when necessary *before* you fall into a rut. This of course requires you to recognize that something that once worked no longer does, which unfortunately does not always happen easily or right away. People instead often exert even more effort in an attempt to obtain the same outcome as before. However, the desired outcome will never occur in the intended manner once conditions have changed. What was rewarded in the past may no longer work or be valued. Instead of quickly changing the behavior, people do more of it. Remember Ron, who as you learned in "Getting Started" suffered under the changing conditions after he was hired? He entrenched himself in his comfort zone and refused to let go of his old ways.

We can draw upon psychological research to help explain why we continue to act in the same way even though we know conditions have changed. By better understanding this tendency you will be able to recognize its onset, which will in turn put you in a position to better avoid this type of unproductive behavior.

In reinforcement theory there is a phenomenon known as an *extinction burst*. When an extinction burst occurs a person repeatedly tries, unsuccessfully, to do something that worked previously. Think, for instance, about a soda vending machine. You expect it to work and are trained to anticipate the same outcome each time. Simply put in a few quarters, push a button, and a drink comes out. Have you ever watched what people do when it doesn't work? They will look at the machine for a moment, mystified, then push the button again. Nothing. Then they push it again, and then even faster. Still nothing. And they push it again. You get the idea. They repeat the same behavior several times before accepting that the expected outcome is not going to happen. Another easy way to illustrate an extinction burst is with gamblers. Instead of recognizing a loss and walking away, they opt to bet even more in hope of making a bigger gain to recoup their losses.

The same concept applies to your success and even to the success of entire organizations. At work it would be easy for you to repeat the same behavior, just as you would with an extinction burst, because that was what enabled you to be successful in the past. You cannot allow yourself to fall into this trap. There is a quick learning curve with a vending machine, and most people will give up fairly quickly. In your job, however, it will not be as easy to determine that something that once worked is no longer working. Unlike your reaction to a malfunctioning vending machine it may be hard for you to admit that something you once did well may not work in the future. This is especially true when what isn't working is in an area in which you are particularly strong or have received accolades in the past. Don't make this mistake. Do not ever become complacent with the development of your brand and skills. Do not double down, as the losing gambler would, and do more of the same. Instead, redirect your energy and exert those efforts toward doing your next great thing.

THE STAGNATION OF YAHOO!

In the earlier days of the Internet, before Google (BG), people used Yahoo! as their go-to search engine. It was by many accounts the preeminent site on the Internet. By 2012, however, Google—which did not even exist until 1998—had attained a search engine market share of more than 66 percent. To truly understand how significant this is, you need to go back only ten years. In 2004, Yahoo! and Google were essentially tied in online search, with both claiming nearly a 30 percent market share. As you can see in Figure 5-3, the companies have been on different paths ever since. Whereas Yahoo! allowed itself to stagnate, Google kept its appetite for innovation and growth and constantly looked to expand its capabilities and offerings.

Google Maps, Google Earth, Google Images, Google Scholar, and Google Shopping are all examples of a series of user-friendly web services the company developed. The

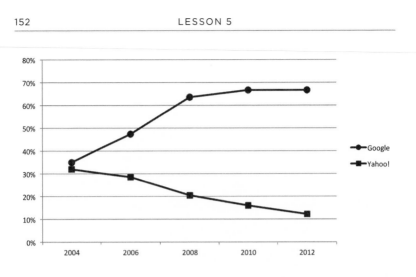

Figure 5-3: Search Engine Market Share

purpose of each of these is to draw users to Google, thereby increasing user traffic and subsequently the opportunity for advertising revenue. Ironically, while doing research for this section of the book I used Google to search for background information about Yahoo!

Examining Figure 5-3 shows you how stagnation can quickly lead to a downward trajectory. From a point of parity in 2004, Google pulled away at an accelerating pace. Yahoo!'s loss literally became Google's gain. If Yahoo! had simply reached a plateau, the company would have maintained its market share of 30 percent. That would not have been entirely bad, especially when put against the comparably small 12 percent market share it had fallen to by 2012. The graph underscores how quickly stagnation can lead to a rapid decline. As with Yahoo!, your decline can be someone else's gain. In this case, Google took advantage of Yahoo!'s complacency and propelled itself into a position as the clear leader. Don't let this kind of situation occur in your career. Always keep in mind that it is important to reinvent your skills and knowledge base. If you don't, you will only be playing catch-up.

You will encounter challenges similar to Yahoo!'s throughout your career. Whether you are at a point of equivalence with others or are much further ahead, constantly maintain vigilance for the next competitor that, like Google, is ready to take your career market share. Career development and growth is constantly ranked in surveys as the most important factor at work for employees—even higher than pay—and you need continual development and growth to avoid stagnation. If you do not do this, you risk ramifications beyond just losing ground against others and stalling your career. An absence of career development can lead to stress and feelings of anxiety, and eventually you may even begin to dread going to work.

CONCLUSION

In many areas of your career a quick recovery from mistakes is possible. For instance, you could go a month or two without receiving feedback (Lesson 1) and you probably would not have done something so drastic that you would be derailed for a long period of time. If you find yourself in the throes of stagnation, however, you will likely have a difficult time digging yourself out. Once you let stagnation set in, the consequences are far reaching and hard to undo. For this reason you must constantly self-assess your skills and progress against your trajectory to keep stagnation from taking hold.

Be out at the front of positive change, and be an advocate of it. You cannot passively sit on the sidelines and wait for change to come to you. Sometimes you will need to go against what feels natural and comfortable. Memorex found comfort in knowing it had success with 14-inch disks. Even though the company knew that the future was moving toward smaller disks—and had built the technology for it—it was slow to break out of its mold and go "all in" on the future. If you are always just putting your toes in the water, you will never be able to go all in with your own career and aspirations.

EXERCISE

Identify a skill that is critical for your job and is one that you feel
is a personal strength. This should be the skill that differentiates
you the most from others. Think back to when you first started
your job and how accomplished you were with this skill at that
time. Does this skill matter as much now as it did then? Do you
still have the same competitive advantage with this skill when
compared to your peers? If not, what do you need to do in order
to get the advantage back? Write down your answers on the
Notes page and then list any new skills that you need to acquire
in order to immediately develop and grow.

NOTES

ACHIEVING GROWTH FROM FAILURE

Success is not final, failure is not fatal:

it is the courage to continue that counts.

—WINSTON CHURCHILL

At this point you may be wondering about the old adage that failure breeds success, and what the implications of that are to your trajectory. Surely failure must involve a downward trajectory. However, before making such a sweeping assertion it's helpful to first understand the mechanisms that surround situations of failure. As long as you can take positive learnings away from a failure, you will be able to recover sooner than you otherwise would and in turn keep the situation from resulting in a sustained downward trajectory. In fact, if you use the lessons from your failure to build new knowledge and better prepare, it becomes *constructive failure,* which can lead to an even steeper upward trajectory thereafter.

Thomas Edison is often used as an example of someone who failed many times in his endeavors. When he did not succeed with one approach, he was a master of turning it into a constructive failure. He is well known for the positive and optimistic way in which he viewed failure. Whereas people say he failed hundreds of times in his quest to invent the light-bulb, he looked at it differently. From Edison's standpoint, something that did not work was one more approach that he could cross off his list as "proven not to work" for the light-bulb. Every time he could eliminate a failure he knew he was one step closer to success. His words of wisdom still apply today: "If I find 10,000 ways something won't work, I haven't failed. I am not discouraged, because every wrong attempt discarded is another step forward." Put another way, he viewed every unsuccessful attempt as progress in his trajectory to invent a working lightbulb.

The way that you must view failure is very similar to what you learned in Lesson 1 in regard to the way you must view feedback: You have to depersonalize it. If you fail—and at some point everyone does in some manner—you must not take the failure personally. You should be introspective and learn from it, but you cannot let it drag you down for a sustained period of time. If you overly internalize it or take the failure too personally that is what will happen. You will ruminate on it for too long, which will affect your ability to use it constructively. And it is this result—not the failure itself—that will lead to your trajectory taking a downward path. In a world that moves and advances with such speed, you must be able to quickly learn from mistakes (not just your own, but also the mistakes that others make) in order to increase your chances of staying ahead.

History is littered with people who are famous for great accomplishments that were borne out of failure. Consider Christopher Columbus, who sought fame and fortune in his adventure on the sea. His goal was to find a path to the East Indies; instead he found a new land in the Americas. Despite proving unsuccessful in his attempt to find a western route to the Orient, history has judged him as a great explorer. Why? Because he changed course based upon new knowledge and events. This new course resulted in forever changing the world.

EVOLUTIONARY UNDERPINNINGS

If you are bothered by failure, you are not alone. Humans are hardwired to have an intrinsic fear of failure. In evolutionary terms this stems from a basic sense of survival. Failure in the most fundamental sense meant no food or shelter; failure came in not securing the necessities to survive. This same principle applies in the modern world. People want to succeed, and they generally want to be recognized for doing so. The opposite applies for failure. People want to avoid it, and when it happens they do not want to be continually reminded of it. When they are, they can quickly learn to feel as if failure is inevitable. When this occurs it becomes harder to persist toward your goals.

In a series of groundbreaking studies, the pioneering psychologist Dr. Martin Seligman explored the conditions that cause people to give up. In the most famous of his experiments he found that when dogs were given an electrical shock, different behaviors would ensue depending on whether or not escape from the shock was possible. In what he termed *learned helplessness*, a dog that could not find a way to escape would give up hope and stop exploring ways to get out. The dog felt that nothing it could do would change the situation and subsequently stopped trying. Interestingly, the principles behind this concept are the reason why the modern-day invisible dog fence can still be effective when it is turned off. Once a dog has been trained to know how far it can go before it is shocked, it will likely not try to go past that point even if the fence is turned off or broken.

When learned helplessness occurs, an individual has developed an expectation that certain outcomes are beyond personal control. This phenomenon is especially dangerous in humans, as it results in a surrendering of control. If you develop learned helplessness you have made a decision that other factors and people will determine your success. This causes you to deflect the source of your problem to others or to the situation you are in. In making this faulty attribution to external causes it becomes even harder to convince yourself to change for the positive. In reality, success is a choice. Your choice. Almost anything that matters is a choice. You should choose every day to be the best that you can, and in doing so will be able to control your trajectory.

The connection between learned helplessness and failure is based on the fact that success is a choice. When it comes to learned helplessness you can do one of two things: You can develop learned helplessness when conditions change and tell yourself that there is nothing that you can do about it, or you can do something about it and continue to evolve and build your skills to avoid failure. While learned helplessness is an area with a negative outcome, Seligman's research also addresses a positive outcome that can manifest instead. This phenomenon, which is known as *learned optimism*, results in a sense of belief within yourself that you will succeed in an endeavor. Just as you can learn to accept failure, you can learn to expect success. As you will see in Lesson 7, research shows that this expectation of positive outcomes will lead to more success.

As Edison did after each failure, you should reevaluate situations to see if circumstances have changed. Through re-evaluation of a situation you can learn from your mistakes and not let failure prevent you from trying again. The fact that something did not work in the past does not guarantee that it or something similar won't work in the future. Sometimes conditions change. Something that was once met with skepticism may now be met with applause.

Humans are naturally disposed to "escape" from failure because of the fact that in evolutionary terms it could amount to death. While in most cases the consequences are no longer as severe, we still have a difficult time with failure and sometimes give up too easily. Because of the extreme outcomes that can result, our brains are wired in such a way that we process and store negative information much faster than we do positive information. This creates what is known as a *negativity bias*, wherein the effect of a bad outcome more powerfully drives our mindset than does the effect of a good outcome.

Based on the historically harsh consequences of failure, it is evolutionarily adaptive for bad events to have a more lasting impact on us than do good events. Because of this the effects of a good outcome generally dissipate faster than the effects of bad events. Put another way, bad will stay with you longer. Others also will remember it longer. It is therefore incumbent on you to undo your most severe failures as quickly as possible. It has been estimated that we need at least five positive situations to offset one negative situation. To counteract this you need to seek ways to create more good than bad to balance the outsized strength of the latter.

If you fear failure you will also begin to limit your creativity and risk-taking—your willingness to think big, which we discussed in Lesson 3. And when you fear failure you also will begin to procrastinate. All of this occurs in an attempt to try to delay or avoid what you view as a possible failure. While you can always learn from failure, not all failures are created equally—some are more severe. Failure can be broken into three categories: (1) preventable failures, (2) unavoidable failures in complex systems, and (3) intelligent failures at the frontier. The preventable failures will have the worst impact on your career. For example, your team was waiting to receive a file by the end of the day, and you forgot to send it. As a result, they were not able to finish their work and a key milestone was missed. The only lesson to learn from this is to not do it again; should you forget something like that another time you will quickly lose trust and credibility. The other two types of failures are trickier, and your positive response remains essential.

When failure is driven by complexity in an area of uncertainty you have a chance to pull very important lessons from it. Nobody could have fully prepared for the tremendous damage and loss of life that occurred when the World Trade Center towers collapsed in New York during the 9/11 attacks. During this chaotic event a very complex emergency response effort ensued, one that had no precedent. One of the major obstacles encountered by first responders was an inability to communicate with each other. Among the many problems were communications systems that were overwhelmed because of the massive number of people trying to use the networks, and a lack of interoperability across first responders (most were on different systems that did not allow communications across the multiple agencies). Even though progress has been made in making improvements based on this unavoidable failure in a complex system, even now there are necessary fixes that have not been made.

The third type of failure, intelligent failure on the frontier, is often referred to as good failure. The reason is that the area in which the failure occurred is so new that the lessons from it can be drawn upon to make large improvements. This type of failure is based on an event or situation that has not been encountered before. Experimenting with new medical drugs, trying to create a new product, or making a large shift in direction at your company into a new area (blue ocean) would all be examples. Because this is uncharted territory, sometimes even a success is initially disguised as a failure. Thomas Edison's efforts provide an example here too. Early in his career Edison struggled to invent a product that he could bring to the market as a commercial success. He thought he had finally found it after he created the first electronic method for gathering votes during elections. He was fairly certain that this would revolutionize the voting process and be the way of the future. The problem is that it was not seen as such then. People still had a general distrust of such capability and preferred to cast ballots the traditional way. Now, of course, all modern elections use electronic voting methods in some capacity.

UNCOVER THE POSITIVE

The most important aspect of failure is to do everything you can to pull out the positive from the situation and then set out to find a way to use it constructively. In fact, this might even lead you to do something that you thought was not possible, or think of something you had not thought of before. This applies whether the failure is self-induced or brought on by something outside of your control. Amadeo Giannini, the founder of what became Bank of America, experienced both failure and extraordinary success. He is a profound example of someone who had to look really deep to find the positive after a series of horrific events. One of his biggest "failures" was in fact based on events entirely outside of his control.

Giannini opened his first bank in San Francisco in 1904, at a time when it was very difficult for the common person to get a loan at a decent interest rate. At the turn of the twentieth century, loans with good rates were still something reserved for the wealthy. Giannini saw the best in people and believed that the lower and middle classes would be responsible and pay back their loans. He decided to chart a course into this untapped blue ocean, which is a concept we discussed in Lesson 4.

Many of you may be familiar with the earthquake and subsequent fires in San Francisco in 1906. These had a devastating effect on the city, killing roughly 3,000 people and wiping out nearly all of the homes and businesses. Included in the earthquake's destruction was Giannini's bank building. Instead of dwelling on this loss Giannini jumped into action and in doing so capitalized on what was a very difficult situation for his business. Just as he had taken a risk on a previously underserved population, he again took a risk after the earthquake and did something different. Unlike the big bankers, who wanted to remain closed to further evaluate the situation, Giannini realized that people would now more than ever need access to money. Recognizing this need, he raced to the ruins of his bank and was able to remove the money from the vaults before the heat from the approaching fire made doing so impossible. He then made the decision to set up his bank outdoors to provide customers much-needed access to money. Doing this built even more trust and brought in new customers to his bank.

Nobody is advocating that failure is optimal—simply that it does not have to be negative. This requires a strong level of understanding and resiliency. When Giannini considered the implications afterward of not having a banking system, he realized that banking could serve a positive function and be empowering to individuals. From this he decided to build a network of bank branches, which was a novel approach at the time. This enabled him to take what could have been a permanent disaster and turn it into a key launching point that resulted in his becoming one of the most successful bankers in history.

All too often a key step toward success is disguised as failure. If you do not seek to understand the situation better you may miss the hidden success within. Sometimes what seems to be a disaster can actually become the beginning of a strong foundation. What looks like a loss or failure is only seen as such because more time or insight is needed to understand how to grow from it. Silly Putty, penicillin, Post-it Notes, and many other products were actually inventions that came out of mistakes or failures. It was only afterward that these mistakes were turned into gems and became massive successes.

INTROSPECTION

Introspection is a critical component of learning from failure. Hindsight is of course 20/20, but it also serves as a point of learning. If past is prologue, then you must learn to use your past—including failure—to write what happens next. If you have the right mindset and choose to view the situation as an important event to learn from, you will be able to turn failure on its head. To make this happen you must seek to fully understand what led to the failure. And this will normally be difficult to do.

While failure is often inevitable, at times you will need to acknowledge that it may have resulted from your own shortcomings. The sooner you accept that fact the faster you can turn to seeking solutions to avoid it in the future. That is what matters. Can it be salvaged? Can you do better next time? Is there another way to approach the situation? Through asking yourself a series of evaluative questions such as these you will more quickly get to the root cause and create a new plan.

When failure does occur it is important to not dwell on it for too long. Once you have assessed the situation and determined a plan of action, put it behind you and move on. Ruminating over it can have severe negative consequences and lead your trajectory downward. Do not play the victim and look for nonconstructive excuses or lay blame with others. Do not waste time trying to redirect blame or find a scapegoat. Instead quickly learn from your missteps and move on. A misstep can be just that: You missed a step—you did not fall off of a cliff. Place your next foot back in the right place and you can continue on again. In fact, the further on you continue the less important the failure will seem. At some point you may even find yourself laughing at something you once deemed very dire.

You should also bear in mind that failure is not always incontrovertible failure, even though it may seem that it is. Sometimes it is just failure in someone else's eyes. At other times, as with Edison and his electronic voting machine, it is a success that just takes longer to manifest. In reality, failure is often nothing more than a temporary roadblock. John Grisham received a seemingly countless number of rejections for his first book, *A Time to Kill*. While he is now a globally renowned author, his first book was for all intents a commercial failure at the time it was published. It was only after the publication of his second book, *The Firm*, that his career took off. Incidentally, Grisham himself had a career trajectory that changed considerably based on events in his life. During a trial at the courthouse one day he overheard testimony from a twelve-year-old victim that stuck with him. He began to wonder what would have happened if the child's father had murdered those who assaulted her. From there he began to write his first book. He took a risk that had a chance of failure, and went from being a successful practicing attorney to becoming one of the bestselling authors of all time.

THE FALLACY OF INEVITABLE FAILURE

One of the worst things you can do to harm your trajectory is to avoid taking certain risks because of what you perceive to be the inevitability of failure. One of the greatest military successes in the history of the United States was chalked up in advance as a probable death sentence for those who were to take part in the mission. If the people involved had believed that failure was the only option, success would have been considerably less likely. I am referring to the Doolittle Raid on Japan during World War II. All of the crew members realized that even though the chance of failure was high, it was not a certainty. And the mission was the right thing to do.

The events transpired on April 18, 1942, when a total of sixteen bombers, each with a five-man crew, took off from the USS *Hornet* aircraft carrier in the western Pacific Ocean. This was the beginning of what would turn into one of the biggest surprises of the war and a key turning point in the United States' involvement in it. Amazingly, every crewmember volunteered despite knowing that this mission would include a guaranteed element of failure, along with a high probability of dying.

The known failure was that the aircraft would not have sufficient fuel to return to the USS *Hornet* for a safe landing. Instead, the bombers would continue on to designated safe zones in China after the raid. A further risk developed when the task force that included the USS *Hornet* was sighted by a Japanese boat that quickly radioed its headquarters. As a result the bombers had to take off sooner than expected, which added miles to their trip. After dropping the bombs the crews soon realized that they were not likely to make it to the safe zones because fuel was running low and the weather was worsening. Rather than bailing out over China, fifteen of the planes crash-landed along the coast and the sixteenth landed in Russia; incredibly, most of the airmen survived.

Lieutenant Colonel Doolittle himself thought the raid was a failure after it was over because all sixteen aircraft were lost and only minimal damage was inflicted on the Japanese targets. But remember, failure is relative. Instead of this being a failure, it provided a massive psychological boost to the U.S. troops. And it had another psychological effect: For the first time, it caused Japanese military leaders to question their infallibility.

Unlike the Doolittle Raiders, all of whom were brave volunteers who disregarded the possibility of failure, people in the workplace far too often choose not to try something because they believe that failure is likely. I recall the disappointment in my coworker Ed's eyes one day when he walked into my office and sat down despondently. He proceeded to tell me that he couldn't believe someone else had just taken his idea and received a great response after sharing it with leadership. As he walked me through it I could easily see why the suggestions were received favorably. I then asked why someone else had presented it if it was his idea.

While it took him a while to get to the heart of the matter, the reason he eventually came around to was that he was not sure the idea would be accepted—he feared that it might be rejected. He feared failure and in doing so failed to act. Because we so strongly remember negative events, it is important to realize how long not acting will remain rooted in your memory. Trying something and failing tends to become a fleeting memory over time when you are able to follow the failure with success. When you don't even try something, however, you are left with regret over not knowing what might have happened. If you try but fail you know what happened, and you can learn from it and move on. Fortunately, Ed was able to play a key role in the project and felt that he was still connected to his idea. He even helped refine and improve it. All too often, though, you never get that chance and will wonder what could have been if you only would have tried.

THE HALF-EMPTY *AND* HALF-FULL GLASS

When you are considering whether to pursue something, you need to ensure that there is some realism to the pursuit. To maximize your likelihood of success it helps to consider the challenge from two perspectives. Looking at it from the lens of the glass being half empty will enable you to identify in advance those obstacles that could lead to failure down the road. Don't filter out information that is inconsistent with what you want an outcome to be; if you do you will likely overlook something that's important. Through identifying obstacles you can find ways to mitigate those challenges. You also need to consider your effort from the perspective of the glass being half full. As we will review in more detail in Lesson 7, this positive expectancy is critically important and will improve your chances of succeeding. When you view goals using this dual approach you create a situation in which you are able to change from a "yes, but" to a "yes, if" mindset. One of the worst things you can do is only focus on the glass being half empty, because all you will glean from that is a series of excuses and "yes, but" challenges.

For example, an effort is under way to send a two-person team (one man and one woman) to orbit Mars in January of 2018. This requires studying and learning from a whole host of prior failures and challenges with space flight endeavors. If this were the only focus, however, you would hear nothing but statements such as "Yes, it would be a great mission, but it's too far"; "Yes, we could build the right spacecraft, but it would be too expensive." The organizers of the mission are aware of the risk and even embracing it because they know they can learn from the past and then hopefully do something no one else has ever done. As the organizers state, "These are exactly the kinds of risks that America should be willing to take in order to advance our knowledge, experience and position as a world leader. We believe the risks and challenges we have uncovered are well within the scope of our collective experience and can be overcome."

When you also focus on the glass being half full you create the necessary positive expectancy and begin to hear statements like "Yes, we can do that if we are able to build an environment in the spacecraft that provides basic comforts for such a long journey"; "Yes, we will be able to do it by determining when Mars is closet to Earth."

All of us have natural tendencies to which we are disposed when we act. This will in part determine how you view situations. In this lesson we can't dive deeply into the psychological profiles behind different style preferences, but you still can easily bring to mind people you know in some of the key categories. For example, some people are idea generators.

This is the person who is always coming to you with the next "great invention" or idea. Others prefer to refine and improve existing ideas. When you tell these people about an idea they will immediately jump to thinking of ways to make it even better. Another type of person likes to sell the ideas and get people to buy into the mission. Yet another group of people likes to take ideas that are ready to go and find ways to execute and bring them to fruition.

To help you in your own efforts you should determine which of those categories most closely resembles your style. Then find people in the other categories to help round out your idea to improve the chance of it becoming a resounding success. For example, if you are an idea generator you will side toward a "glass is half full" mentality and should pull in a refiner (who will see the glass as half empty) to help you find ways to improve the idea. In doing so you will reduce your chance of failure by eliminating some of the potential issues up front.

CASCADING FAILURE

During August of 2003 more than 50 million people in the United States experienced a power outage—on the same day! What turned into a miserable experience for so many during the late summer heat was all started by what could have been a very manageable situation. In Northern Ohio an electrical line sagged due to the excessive heat, and a normal control alarm failed to trigger. With no place for the electricity to go, it was transferred to another line, and then another. Then those failed. The electricity had to be transferred to yet more lines, and the problem continued to spread. By the time the flow of electrical failures was halted, people across eight states and Canada were impacted.

A situation such as this is known as *cascading failure*, which occurs when failure spreads across a series of interconnected systems. Because electrical grids are physically connected, the discussion of cascading failure is often confined to networks such as that and computer systems. However, there are many other real-life situations in which one small failure is compounded by another and then another, and so on. These successive failures then lead to a massive failure.

The Air France Concorde disaster in 2000, in which more than 100 people were killed, is another example. Just five minutes before the Concorde departed from Charles de Gaulle International Airport in France, a DC-10 took off from the same runway and a small metal strip fell off of it—a metal strip that came loose due to sloppy installation by mechanics. During takeoff one of the tires on the Concorde hit the metal strip, causing the tire to burst. From the burst a piece of rubber flew upward and struck the wing in its weakest spot, rupturing one of the plane's fuel tanks. There is speculation that because the plane was slightly overloaded and the weight aboard the plane wasn't properly centered, excessive fuel may have been shifted to that fuel tank during taxiing, placing it under more pressure than normal. From the fuel leak a fire started that triggered a loss of power in two of the engines. Damage also prevented the landing gear from being able to retract. The lack of full thrust caused by the loss of engine power combined with the landing gear being stuck limited the plane's ability to climb or gain speed. It crashed into a hotel, killing all 109 people on board and four more on the ground.

The accident investigation revealed that in twenty-seven years of service there were fifty-seven prior recorded incidents of tire bursts on a Concorde, nineteen of which were caused by hitting objects on the ground. In none of these instances did the fuel tank rupture and catch fire. As is the case with cascading failure, one of the worst aspects of the Concorde disaster is that no single event by itself likely would have resulted in a crash. It was only the sequence of events—the cascading failure—that led to the tragic outcome.

While these two examples are used to illustrate cascading failure in an extreme sense, examples abound at work as well. One of the most recent ones that played out publicly involved Ron Johnson, the now former CEO of the retail chain J. C. Penney. In prior roles he was instrumental in the success of rebranding Target, and had served as a highly regarded senior executive at Apple. Johnson had the pedigree to succeed, yet he did not. In just a year and a half with Johnson at the helm the company dropped $4 billion in revenue!

His goal was to turn J. C. Penney around and reshape the retail industry with his new strategy, which was based on a store-within-a-store concept that assumed shoppers would want to hang out and buy merchandise that was not on sale. The problem was that it was *his* strategy. He was largely unconcerned with what others thought or the customer wanted.

Instead of following the think big, act small, move quick strategy (Lesson 3), Johnson tried to do everything at once. He did not start small and then learn, adjust, and expand. His failure to do so compounded bad decisions, because once something was rolled out to all of the stores it was hard to make adjustments.

Business minds will be analyzing and creating case studies on this for years, but perhaps Johnson's biggest failure was his reluctance to listen to feedback, which as you learned in Lesson 1 is critical to success. He felt that because something worked in his past jobs it would of course also work at J. C. Penney. He made a cardinal mistake we discussed in Lessons 4 and 5: He assumed that something that worked before would continue to work. When he replaced most of the executive team with colleagues from his prior company who thought the way he thought, he compounded matters by creating a structure in which it was almost impossible to receive real feedback. When people did have a different opinion he rarely listened and referred to them as skeptics. What he wanted were believers. In effect, he let what could have been small, manageable failures turn into a large cascading failure from which he could not recover.

To avoid triggering your own cascading failure you need to treat failure as a finite event, albeit one that you learn from. If you can avoid committing a series of mistakes in succession, you will greatly limit the risk of the failure bringing down both you and your trajectory. Failure by itself, then, is not the problem. Failure is inevitable. Your response to it is not. The problem lies either in not learning from failure—

and not learning from it quickly enough—or in allowing it to cascade until you are left with a massive problem. When you train yourself to learn quickly from failure you will move more rapidly into new successes, and then again into more.

The importance of following failure with success is supported by recent research that tracked 238 working professionals (across seven companies and three industries) for about four months. The participants were asked to keep individual work diaries in which they would record their responses to questions relating to various situations that occurred. At the end of every day each participant was asked to briefly describe one event that really stood out in his or her mind. It turns out that the best days people had were those days when they felt that progress—even if mundane—was made (i.e., a positive outcome occurred). Not surprisingly, the worst days were those during which a failure or setback occurred. The importance of the small wins is referred to as the *progress principle.* The researchers found that the most important indicator of good performance was the feeling of making meaningful progress. And they also found that the negativity bias again held. Minor failures were found to be influential and more powerful than were positive outcomes.

Creating these successes quickly after failure will make it immensely easier for you to recover from the event and put it behind you. Had J. C. Penney had more positive outcomes during its turnaround effort—even small ones—there would have been a better chance to gain momentum. Instead Johnson's strategy drove down morale and engagement, and the negative continually outweighed the positive.

TRY NEW THINGS

Through positive failure you will generate great insights and learnings. Ironically, those who are most open to new ideas are apt to have more failures over time. Those failures are not caused solely by personal mistakes, but more often by a willingness to experiment and try new ways of doing things. Research conducted by Lewis Goldberg delineated five core characteristics that can be used to define your general stylistic preferences and personality.

Briefly, the first of these is *conscientiousness*, which is based on a person's degree of thoroughness, reliability, and carefulness. The second, *extraversion*, relates to a person's outgoing nature, assertiveness, and desire to seek high levels of stimulation. The next one is *agreeableness*, which is based on being cooperative, kind, and generally trusting of others. The fourth characteristic, *emotional stability*, relates to managing one's reactions, remaining calm, and avoiding temperamental behavior. The last one is referred to as *openness to experience*. This is about willingness to learn; a desire to try new things; imagination, curiosity, and creativity.

In a study of 129 newly hired college graduates, openness to experiment was found to be a very important factor in determining their subsequent career trajectories. What the researchers found was that as the openness of the employees in the study increased, the rate at which performance declined slowed down. As you now know, almost everyone experiences a plateau at some point, and during this time performance diminishes. This is expected, and a career trajectory will likely not always point sharply upward. By being open to trying new things the employees were able to delay the onset of some of the inevitable performance decline. In other words, their trajectory remained higher for longer.

You will recall from Lesson 5 that Netflix found a blue ocean and became a dominant player in a new market. Something that the company is not as frequently touted for, however, is the way it responds to failure. While Netflix continues to break new ground, it has had plenty of failures, many of them public. The key is how the company reacted: It course-corrected. And in one very public instance it did something that is even harder for many: It apologized. When you make a mistake do not double down on it and further compound the problem. If you know you are wrong just admit it and then move forward as quickly as possible. Denying it or prolonging the issue will only leave you further behind.

CONCLUSION

Failure is often perceived as something that went wrong, something for which the outcome should have been more positive. In reality there is a worse failure: failing to try something important because of fear. When you learn to accept failure as a possibility it will open the door for massive success because you will no longer need to constrain yourself to small thinking. When you fear failure you hold back. The best way to not fear failure is to accept it and learn to identify the lessons within it that you will avoid in the future. Though it may not seem like it at the time, failure results in the acquisition of character if you can harness and learn from what went wrong. People remember character. Failure itself can be fleeting, but people will remember how you react to it and bounce back from it. In addition, when you bounce back quickly you will avoid stagnation. Unlike stagnation, which often becomes continual, failure can occur at a single point in time that you quickly move past.

Like pain from an injury, failure is not permanent. It is a temporary state. It certainly will not always feel that way in the moment, but when you look back you will realize that the magnitude seems to diminish over time. Consider that there is probably no failure that is more public than losing the U.S. presidential election as hundreds of millions of people are watching. Yet even these powerful individuals look back on the situation with a positive mindset once the emotion of the situation passes. Al Gore received more popular votes in the 2000 election than did George W. Bush, but because he had fewer electoral votes he did not win the tightest race in history. He could have withdrawn and sulked in his failure. He chose to pursue a different passion and trajectory by focusing on environmental causes. Not only did he find his cause, he made millions of dollars and found fulfillment in the process.

EXERCISE

Think of the last time you failed in something—the bigger the better. Under each of the columns in the following table fill in what you remember about the failure. Use your completed table to remind yourself not to make the same or similar mistakes in the future.

How I Reacted	What I Did	What I Learned	What I Should Have Done Differently

NOTES

SUSTAINING OUTLIER PERFORMANCE

The price of success is hard work, dedication to the job
at hand, and the determination that whether we win or lose,
we have applied the best of ourselves to the task at hand.

—VINCE LOMBARDI

B y now you have learned about factors that can either
enable or derail your trajectory. Through an awareness
of these you are already in a better position to reach the goals
you have set along your trajectory. To attain your goals and
achieve true success you must begin to tie your experiences
together in such a way that you will reach a point of *sustained
performance* over time. Doing so will make you a *positive
outlier*—someone who stands out from the crowd at work
and in life. In statistics an outlier is defined as a data point
that is substantially different from the others. It can be
considered as something that lies outside most of the other

values. When you become an outlier you stick out. And you can do so in a positive way.

To maintain a long track record of success you must not become rigid with what you know and what you do. This is quite important as it relates to your trajectory. If you are rigid you will not be able to see when you should take a detour, use a wise shortcut, or perhaps even change your targeted destination entirely. This may be hard for you to notice because rigidity is not always a conscious state—people can erroneously think that they are adaptable and open to new ideas. Recall from Lesson 1 that proactively seeking feedback is essential. Along with many other benefits, doing this will allow you to avoid unconsciously becoming rigid and set in your ways. It is feedback that opens your eyes and serves as a catalyst to positive change. What you think you want or desire can change. Along your journey you must continually reevaluate what you are doing and what matters to you.

You may not always succeed at being *the best*, but you can succeed at being *your best*. There is a big difference between the two. People expect the latter, not the former. As long as you put forward your full effort you will reach more of your goals and be recognized for your achievements. When you continually persist in doing your best you will over time accrue sustained performance—performance that when viewed in its entirety will be among the best.

As we reviewed earlier, General Electric (GE) is not just the longest-serving company in the Dow Jones Industrial Average, it is the only company that was part of the index when it was created. GE has not maintained this distinction by accident. Sustained performance at any level is never attained over time by accident. From its early days GE constantly sought to break new ground and do what others had not. So much attention is given to Jack Welch and the modern management philosophy of GE that it is easy to forget who founded the company. It was actually Thomas Edison. Yes, the same pioneer who invented the lightbulb was responsible for starting one of the world's most successful companies—a company with sustained performance. The innovation that continues at GE to this day has added to Edison's ongoing legacy.

VISUALIZE YOUR SUCCESS

Just as GE has driven its own sustained performance, you control your own success. It is important to underscore this: You have even more control than you might think. By simply believing deeply in yourself and your own capabilities you will be significantly more likely to accomplish what you seek. You must be aware of the fact that you can unconsciously be your best advocate or your own biggest obstacle. You can use the experiences in your history to your advantage or detriment, depending on how you allow yourself to interpret the past. There is a critical need for you to deeply believe that your success is achievable and imminent. By being realistic—but optimistic—you will increase the likelihood of succeeding.

At this point you are probably asking, "But how do I do that?" It can be done through nothing more than the power of thought and positive belief. Visualization of an outcome is one technique that can assist you in reaching the goals you have set along your trajectory. Picture your golf ball landing close to the flag on the green, picture the crowd at the opening of your first restaurant, picture the new office you will move into when you receive the promotion you have been working toward.

Emmitt Smith stated that when he was in the NFL he spent so much time visualizing holes in the opposing football team's defense that sometimes he would run with his eyes closed to see if he could hit one. Michael Jordan once famously shot and made a free throw during a basketball game with his eyes closed. A popular legend tells of Major James Nesmeth, who was a prisoner of war during Vietnam. According to the story he was held captive by the enemy for a grueling seven years. During this time he mentally played golf on his home course every day. He did not just visualize a good shot. He visualized driving to the course, putting his shoes on, picking up his tee after a shot, the smell of the course. Amazingly, Major Nesmeth visualized playing the course at a normal speed. During his imprisonment he would spend hours at a time imagining himself playing a great round. What did he do upon his release? Major Nesmeth promptly proceeded to play the best round of his life! Although this particular story may be more legend than fact, the technique does work. Try it some time. Seriously. It can work for you too. Do it for bowling, or for the big speech you have coming up. Better yet, do it anytime you are anxious about an upcoming event or activity.

If you are still wondering whether visualization is a good use of your time, consider this scenario: You are training for the Olympics and your coach allows you to choose to be in one of four training groups. You could be in Group A and follow a traditional regime with 100 percent physical practice. Group B would be 75 percent physical and 25 percent mental. Group C would split at 50 percent physical and 50 percent mental. Finally, Group D would be 75 percent mental and 25 percent physical practice. Think about this for a moment. Which would you choose?

In advance of the 1980 Olympics the Russians purportedly tested this by placing athletes in the four different groups. Astoundingly, it was the athletes in Group D who won the most medals. What scientists have found is that your central nervous system (CNS) is not designed to distinguish between real and imagined events. Through imagery and visualization you begin to build confidence and create a conscious memory of how you should react in a given situation. This in turn trains your CNS to follow the pattern that you have ingrained in your mind.

More recent proof can be found in the success of Michael Phelps, the eighteen-time Olympic gold medalist. Although Phelps does possess amazing physical skills and followed a well-documented rigorous training schedule, his coach, Bob Bowman, indicated that it was mental preparation that truly set him apart. Bowman stated, "He's the best I've ever seen, and he may be the best ever, in terms of visualization. He will see exactly the perfect race and he will see it like he's sitting in the stands, and he'll see it in the water. And then he will go through scenarios—what if things don't go well? Like if his suit rips or his goggles break. And then he has this database, so that when he swims the race he's already programmed his nervous system to do one of those. And he'll just pick the one that happens to come up. If everything is perfect, he'll just go with the perfect one; if he's got to make a change, he's already got it in there." His Olympic success further underscores how you can use this technique and the value of doing so.

In addition to visualizing the best-case scenarios, Phelps also visualized and prepared for alternative and worst-case scenarios. As Bowman mentioned, Phelps was then able to respond so much quicker because he had programmed himself and his CNS to be ready for the other options. Applying this technique to the workplace, consider a presentation in which you are not sure how the audience will react. Might you need to change the focus of the talk slightly? Perhaps insert a few jokes to lighten the mood? Answer unexpected questions? You will not know in advance exactly what will occur, but you can increase your chances of responding to any of the scenarios or questions posed by vividly playing out each one in your head in advance. Or consider an important interview you have coming up. You can prepare responses to common interview questions and then visualize yourself sitting in the room and answering the questions. The closer you can get to visualizing the real-life scenario, the better positioned you will be to perform well and get the job.

BELIEVE YOUR SUCCESS

Through visualization you will perform better and thereby increase your confidence. This builds what is known as *self-efficacy*, which is the belief you have within yourself that you will succeed in what you are doing. Study after study has scientifically shown the importance of a person's mindset in achieving success in every type of endeavor imaginable. Put simply, if you think you will do well, you will do better than you would if you think you will fail. Research on self-efficacy has revealed to us that it is absolutely essential that you believe in yourself. When you have low self-efficacy you will have very little confidence in your own ability to succeed and reach your goals. If you have high self-efficacy you will be just the opposite: You will have strong self-confidence and believe in the high probability of succeeding in what you do.

In a series of milestone studies in this area, Dr. Albert Bandura sought to assess participants' levels of self-efficacy in tasks that were then measured for performance. What he found was that the groups that included people with low self-efficacy performed worse than those with average self-efficacy, who in turn performed worse than those with the highest levels. While this may seem discouraging for anyone with low self-efficacy, there is great news. Studies have also found that self-efficacy can be raised. When that occurs, the same person would then do better. This is such an important but often overlooked finding within the research. Self-efficacy is not innate. So many characteristics are next to impossible to change, but self-efficacy is not; you can increase it through practice and repetition. When you consider the implications of this for your career it should quickly become clear that you need to generate successes. You need to do so not only for the sake of success itself, but also for the essential by-product of maintaining and growing your own self-efficacy. By setting goals you will reach them and then begin to feel more and more confident as the magnitude of your goals and aspirations increases.

Just as success breeds success, high self-efficacy begets more self-efficacy, which enables you to better cope with failure. You are able to do so because people who have strong self-efficacy recognize that failure is temporary and success will soon follow. Failure, which we discussed in more detail in Lesson 6, will always happen to some degree. What is most important is that you are equipped to handle it when it does. Another positive by-product found in people who have high self-efficacy is persistence. As a result they are less prone to give up because they know that they will reach the goal if they are tenacious and keep at it. Higher levels of self-efficacy will even lower stress because you will be more comfortable and confident. That in turn will reduce anxiety, which is one of the main causes of stress.

When we trace self-efficacy back to goal setting, which we discussed in Lesson 3, an exciting implication emerges: The more you believe in yourself, the more ambitious you become with the goals you are willing to set and take on. In other words, as your self-efficacy grows so too will your willingness to think big. Let's say you want to learn to swim. Surely you are not going to try to swim across a lake right away. But as you reach your first goal of learning to float, and then your second to tread water, and then to swim a short distance and so on, you will build your self-efficacy as it relates to swimming. Before long, swimming across a lake—something that once seemed unimaginable—quickly becomes a goal you will feel comfortable setting and reaching.

As your self-efficacy in a given area increases, you will also begin to create a situation in which you can embolden a *self-fulfilling prophecy*. Whereas self-efficacy is based on your own sense of confidence that you can do something, a self-fulfilling prophecy (SFP) is a belief that an outcome will happen because you and others act in advance as though it is a foregone conclusion. When others expect someone to do well, they act as if they expect the person to succeed, leading the person to behave in a manner that tries to fulfill those expectations.

In tests of the SFP, the psychologist Robert Rosenthal found very striking results. In the most famous of these studies he partnered with an elementary school to determine whether teachers' expectations of students would influence subsequent performance. For the purposes of the study the teachers were intentionally misled and given expectations about students when classes began. They were told that based on the results of an IQ test, certain students could be expected to do much better in school. In what he termed the *Pygmalion effect*, Rosenthal found that those same students scored much better on a follow-up IQ test at the end of the school year than did the other students.

In actuality, the "best" students were picked at random. Rosenthal and his coauthor (Lenore Jacobson, who was the principal at the school) surmised that the teachers' preconceived expectations led them to give more attention to those students. Curiously, the effects were most pronounced for first- and second-grade students. There was not as much of a difference for those in higher grades. The authors speculated that it could have to do with the fact that the teachers had not yet had a chance to form an opinion of the younger students. In other words, the teachers' expectancy was still being formed. They had observed the older students in prior years and had a more thorough understanding of their capabilities. This is a powerful suggestion, and it has immense applicability to those new in their career or starting a new job. It means that you can aid your trajectory simply by starting strong and getting off on the right foot. In doing so you can establish a positive expectancy among your colleagues and superiors.

Negative expectancy effects are all too easy to create when you are not aware of how these things can develop. A student who causes mischief at school quickly becomes tagged as a troublemaker. A minor incident that was committed by a "good" student might cause a teacher to roll her eyes, but the same incident committed by a student who is expected to be "bad" becomes a reason to send the offender to detention again. That student faces a headwind in his or her trajectory. Why? Because the school's teachers become accustomed to an expectation of wrongdoing and are on the lookout for the slightest infraction. It will take a long pattern of good behavior to change the teachers' expectancy for this pupil. It is no different at work. You must not make the little mistakes. Little mistakes create an expectancy of failure and lead to people waiting for even bigger mistakes.

The effects of the self-fulfilling prophecy actually reach beyond individuals and also apply to teams. It is easy to expand this individual effect and spread a type of contagiousness that creates a group SFP. This team-level prophecy is known as the *synergistic accumulative effect.* Our behaviors, attitudes, and actions are all noticed by those with whom we work. Not only are these things noticed, but they also influence others. As you have likely seen, all too often a meeting, party, or other event is completely changed by one person. That person's attitude and excitement can lift up the whole group. On the other hand, that same person can spread a negative attitude that quickly permeates the room. The SFP can be used to raise not only yourself but others. At work as in life, the total is usually more than the sum of its parts. Group self-fulfilling prophecies are even more powerful than individual ones. Lifting those around you will enable you to do even more. Particularly if you lead a team, remember how strongly your attitude and actions will impact others.

Just as they do at the individual level, synergistic accumulative effects can work against you and your team if you are not careful. It is your job to make them work to your advantage. To illustrate what can happen if you don't, consider the Great Depression. The self-fulfilling prophecy of a single person would not have been sufficient to lead to massive failures within the banking system, but a collective prophecy did. After the stock market crashed, word spread that the banks would not be able to pay back people's money. Individuals and soon masses of people all began to believe that the banks were going to fail. This in turn led to these same masses of people running to banks to withdraw their money. Of course, banks invest money and do not keep nearly enough cash on hand to pay everyone back. As the withdrawal requests increased the banks eventually could not keep up, and massive panic ensued.

Collectively the various terms such as Pygmalion effect, self-fulfilling prophecy, and synergistic accumulative effect are all different types of *expectancies.* You can learn to use the power of an expectancy effect to your advantage rather than allow it to work against you, which can happen if you are not careful. When you connect goal theory (Lesson 3) and self-efficacy with expectancy effects, something very powerful emerges. You create a perpetual circle of success, as shown Figure 7-1. What you can see is that each of these will build off of the others. When you set and reach a goal you will build your self-efficacy. As your self-efficacy grows, so too will your willingness to reach for bigger goals. People will notice that and see your success, which leads to their having higher expectations of you. Then you will seek to fulfill those expectations, resulting in your performance growing even more.

Consider this example. You are starting a new job in a different department of your company and have little experience in that aspect of the business. On top of that, the new job is a very visible position and includes significantly more responsibility. Yet deep down you know you will succeed.

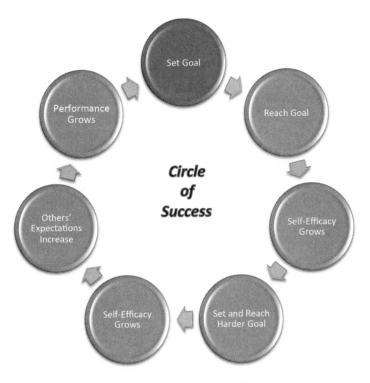

Figure 7-1: Perpetual Circle of Success

This will not be the first time you have taken a risk in moving into a role with which you had only limited familiarity. You know you have created a successful track record that you can build upon and remember, leading you to believe you again will do well.

In addition, you were approached by your new manager about the position based on a conversation she had with your prior boss. You underwent a rigorous interview process and did well throughout. This all leads to your creating a positive expectancy among those with whom you will be working.

The hiring managers and your new colleagues also expect you to do well because of referrals and their own positive interaction with you. Your beliefs coupled with the positive expectancies of others provide a powerful way to start off on the right foot in any situation. Remember, success precipitates success.

When you have built a high level of self-efficacy you will find that there is a connection between your actions and the outcome you want to achieve. Luck is nice to have at times—and even important—but it is neither a strategy nor sustainable. Research on reinforcement has shown that it is essential to be able to find how your behavior influences the outcome. When only luck is involved people quickly give up hope and stop trying. This leads to the feelings of learned helplessness that we covered in Lesson 6. It is important to note that self-efficacy is not a constant across everything you do. Instead it will vary with the task at hand. You can have a great deal of self-efficacy on one thing, but little on another. For instance, you may really believe that you are a great singer but would be absolutely terrified to try to swim. While you can build self-efficacy anywhere, your focus should be primarily on those areas that are most instrumental to your happiness and success.

It bears repeating that you own your trajectory. Others will help, but it is yours to obtain. Because of this simple fact you must view life and its challenges with an *internal locus of control*. People who have an internal locus or center of control believe they are in charge of their own success and take responsibility for it, as well as for their mistakes. When you do this you begin to create the expectancy that you do in fact determine your future. Recall Ron and Cindy, whom you met in Lesson 1. Cindy's actions provide an example of adopting an internal locus of control and steering the situation to one's advantage.

Ron, who had the opposite persona, adopted an *external locus of control*. He blamed others for his circumstances. Instead of looking for ways in which he could work through the new situation he looked for ways to blame others for his problems. Through doing this he gave up in believing in himself. Of course that was not productive, and he ultimately left the organization. When you adopt an external locus of control you divert important energy toward focusing on the wrong things. Instead of focusing on what you can improve and how you can achieve your goals, you spend valuable time searching for external factors and excuses for what went wrong. Moreover, when things go well you may attribute the events to luck instead of giving yourself well-deserved credit for your success. In a much broader sense it is important to realize that the one thing in life you can most control is yourself. You cannot always control your workplace, nor the actions of others. By focusing on your own performance and skill development you will best position yourself for continued growth. Be aware of what others are doing and learn from them, but do not get so caught up with what they are doing that you lose focus on the things you can control.

ENJOY YOUR SUCCESS

Sustaining outlier performance over time is extremely difficult without alignment of your interests and skills with your job. When you consider your desired trajectory you must do so with an awareness of your personality along with your strengths and weaknesses. If you do not account for your natural tendencies and preferences you will be less prepared for what will happen as you proceed through your career and trajectory. For example, if you are generally an introverted person, pursuing a career in sales may not be your best option. Similarly, if you are naturally extraverted you would do best to shy away from a job such as a night watchman.

Interestingly, personality types can even lead to different expected patterns in trajectories. Using the same example of introverted versus extraverted, let's review how trajectories might differ based on personality. Though nothing is 100 percent definitive, extraverts are likely to have more steep spikes, but also sharp drops in their trajectory. Introverts will instead tend to have a more sustained, gradual trajectory. When you look at Figure 7-2, you can see what this can look like. An introvert and extravert may have the same end goal, and both could achieve it. However, their paths could be substantially different along the way.

The reason is that they have different personality preferences, which drive their behavior. Whereas extraverts tend to speak more than listen, introverts are the opposite. Whereas introverts are more cautious and deliberate, extraverts are willing to move faster and take more risks. When you exam-

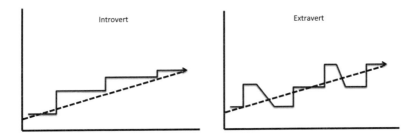

Figure 7-2: Sample Trajectories by Personality Type

ine these two styles it becomes apparent why trajectories can differ. The introvert is less likely to make large mistakes but might miss out on big wins. Similarly, the extravert is more willing to accept and bounce back quickly from failure and might have large victories, but then make a miscalculation and go down before going back up. That would result in a less linear trajectory as compared to an introvert. If you have never done so, I encourage you to take a personality assessment to see where you fall on these and other personality continuums. Many employers have development programs that include one of these assessments, and many versions are also available online at no cost.

By gaining a clearer understanding of your interests and strengths you will be able to focus on those areas and career trajectories in which personal fulfillment and success are most likely. A fundamental mistake that many people make is to spend an inordinate amount of time and energy on improving their weaknesses. While this is important, in some areas of weakness you will only be able to improve so much.

Beyond that you are exerting effort in the pursuit of what is likely to lead to limited incremental improvement. Instead, by blending skills, interests, and aspirations, you will be in a position to build upon your strengths without having to change the essence of what is most important to you. This will lead you toward a career that will be more fulfilling and aligned with your personality preferences.

If you do not align your interests and natural skills in your occupation you will over time become burned out and demotivated. Instead of trying to force yourself to like something, change what you do or how you do it in a way that brings you joy. By changing in this way you are simply adapting, not compromising your innate interests or abilities. This is critical, as almost all sustained success requires change and adaptation. That does not mean, however, that you should try to change everything at once. When you try to do too much at once you can easily find yourself overwhelmed. Moreover, you will likely change a number of things, but only to a minimal degree of success. If you make one key change at a time, you will be able to focus more and your skill and comfort level will quickly expand. Soon, what was once an area outside of your comfort zone will become an area of competence. Like change, your trajectory is best managed through a series of successive and successful steps.

You will find that if you move along in such a manner you will find greater satisfaction and happiness. You must seek to maintain happiness throughout your career and life. Do not compromise it for short-term gain. Many people believe that success leads to happiness. This is proving to be fundamentally inaccurate. In an extensive meta-analysis, researchers found evidence that happiness is a stronger predictor of success than the other way around (meta-analysis is a statistical procedure in which results from many studies are brought together to find out what the "true" relationship is across variables). Our traditional sense of what matters is actually backward.

Shawn Achor expands on this idea in his book *The Happiness Advantage*, where he describes why it is so important to start with happiness. If you start with striving for success before striving for happiness, the goalpost keeps moving. You tell yourself that happiness is right around the corner, but then when you get there you want more. If you can just get that next raise, or big promotion, or whatever it is you think you need—then you will be happy. During the pursuit of success it is easy to sacrifice your happiness because you believe you will get back to it soon. What happens instead is that once you achieve that next success the novelty wears off, just as it does with a new car. After a few miles you already begin thinking about your next new car instead of being happy with the one you have.

Happiness does not result from pursuing success for its own sake. Happiness is better viewed as an outcome of what you will experience when you do something for which you have a great passion. You can sustain performance for a period of time without passion, but eventually it will catch up with you and you will find that your performance diminishes. If you are not happy at work, you are less likely to succeed to your full potential.

Ideally you will be able to find that job that perfectly blends your passions—inside and outside of work—so that you can find flow. Blake Mycoskie, who founded the shoe company TOMS, remarked that his business is the perfect job for him. And this is coming from someone who started five other companies first. The reason? Because at TOMS the job no longer felt like work. He found a way to blend his professional, personal, and philanthropic interests into one harmonious environment (TOMS is famous for donating one pair of shoes to a child in need for every pair purchased). Finding this perfect combination allowed him to concentrate all of his efforts on one mission, and in doing so he created a new intertwined business model combining profit with philanthropic giving.

When you are fully vested in and truly enjoy what you do, you substantially increase the likelihood of it leading to even greater things. Recall Tony Hawk, from Lesson 2. He did not get into skateboarding with the intent of building an empire around his iconic brand, he got into skateboarding because it is what he loves. Through the passion, skill, and persistence he displayed he went on to do things that nobody else had ever done before. Doing so then opened up even more opportunities that he was able to capitalize on.

FILTER THE NOISE

There is so much going on every day. Our worlds never seem to stop moving. You have priorities and commitments at work. At home. At church. At your child's school. Everywhere.

Many of these activities are real priorities, but others are largely just distractions. When you turn on the radio any static you hear in the background is called *noise,* and the words or music you are trying to listen to is the *signal.* When you have too much noise you cannot hear the signal. That is, you cannot focus on what matters most. At work and in life you must separate the signal from all of the noise that surrounds you every day. When you do this you will get rid of "the stuff" that is distracting you and be able to focus on what matters.

We can use a traditional bell curve diagram (Figure 7-3) to demonstrate this point. Generally speaking, a lot of little things add up to a lot of time. The time often adds up because we ruminate over how much we have to do and procrastinate in getting things done. In Figure 7-3, Activity Importance

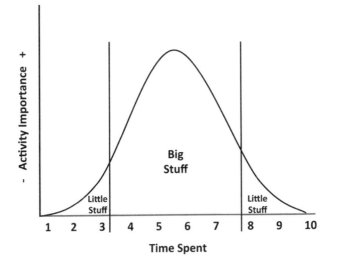

Figure 7-3: The Stuff Curve

and Time Spent are represented along the two axes. You can see that if you have ten hours, it is easy to spend more than half of your time on things that are less important. Look at the proportion of time you are spending on important things (signal) versus unimportant stuff (noise). A simple rule of thumb you can use is that if something will take less than five minutes, do it as soon as possible to get it out of the way. If you do this for an hour you can get twenty little things done quickly, which will drive out unnecessary distractions. By completing these activities you have just freed up your mind to focus on the big things with less distraction.

I am not trying to imply that this is an absolute. Instead what I want you to take away from this is that prioritization is necessary. Little things are important and still need to get done. However, you should not spend more time on those than on the big things that matter and that have the largest impact on success in your life and career. Just as with decision making (Lesson 3), so many times you already know what to do. Do it and then invest your energy on the more important things—the things that will differentiate you in your career.

CONCLUSION

Sustained performance is never easy—but it is attainable. The secret is believing in yourself in order to make it happen. You can make it easier to reach sustained performance by striving to focus on that which gives you the greatest satisfaction. You can continue for a long time doing something successfully at work, but true success will only come when you match what you are doing with what you want to do. Without this match you will eventually feel like you are simply going through the motions, waiting for your real calling to come along. But it is not likely to come along on its own, and you should actively pursue that which you want.

With so much going on at any given time, it is often easy to ignore the little things and deem them inconsequential or irrelevant to your success. While there is an inherent desire for speed, the old saying "haste makes waste" frequently applies. Instead, it is often prudent to "slow down to go faster." What I mean by this is that if you do things properly the first time you will stay on the right trajectory. If you do not, the speed you originally sought will elude you because you will find you need to backtrack. Through taking care in what you do and how you do it you will find that you can move faster than ever.

EXERCISE

In the table on the next page list your top five priorities. These can be at work, outside of work, or both. Next to each indicate how much time you spend on that activity each day. What is your total amount of time? If you add up the total hours you spend at work each week, do you find that you are allocating the right amount of time to your key work activities? When you remove the hours you spend working, how many hours remain to focus on other interests? Are you spending time in areas that are preventing you from focusing on your top priorities? If so, determine how you can reduce time there. In the last column you should then indicate what you will do differently so that you can spend more of your time in the areas that are most important to you.

Top 5 Priorities	Time Spent Each Day (hours)	Changes I Will Make
1.		
2.		
3.		
4.		
5.		
TOTAL TIME SPENT		

NOTES

CONCLUSION

There is really never a true peak or top; there is only a point at which you realize you are content or you walk away. If you follow the lessons in this book you will be able to do either of these at a point of your choosing. You will be successful. You will be fulfilled.

An old Confucian proverb states, "What I hear, I forget. What I see, I remember. What I do, I understand." That applies to this book and its seven lessons. Instead of lengthy chapters, you were provided with quick lessons that you can begin to apply immediately. On the surface, the exercise at the end of each lesson seems straightforward. Do not fall into the trap of thinking it is a waste of time. Far from it: Doing these exercises will awaken a period of discovery that will guide you forward. Real success will occur when you begin to apply the new strategies from each lesson in your life every day.

You should consider this book as the starting point in your journey, where you move past remembering and on to understanding. Reading this book will serve as the beginning for you to establish or reestablish the trajectory you seek. It will provide your foundation moving forward. Goal setting, locus of control, expectancy theory, and all of the other topics covered are not independent phenomena. They work together. When you set goals, you reach goals. When you reach goals, you build confidence and self-efficacy. When others see you succeed, they build an expectancy that you will continue to do so. You will create a very powerful loop to accelerate your trajectory. This is important to remember, because few ideas in this book when standing alone will start you on a path for marked success. That will happen when you understand and apply the many connecting points across all of these areas. Independently each lesson will nudge you forward; collectively they will propel you forward.

The world is full of people who have unorthodox but amazing trajectories. Some follow a straightforward pattern, while others are hard to describe. Our world at work is no longer predictable. It's not enough anymore to just put in your time and wait for a promotion. You will need to make strategic moves in your career. Sometimes this will involve risk. You may even take a new job that in the past would not have been viewed as a true promotion, but that will lead to enhancing your skills dramatically. Opportunities for lateral job changes, moves into other functional areas, and even being offered a job on another continent are all examples of different career steps you may encounter and must be prepared for during your career. Careers are not as predictable or linear as they were in the past. The skills you learned in this book will prepare you to excitedly take on any challenge or opportunity you come across.

This changing landscape of career expectations has made it next to impossible to map out any career trajectory with absolute certainty. Every career will have bumps and surprises along the way. By building a plan for your trajectory, though, you can mitigate those problems by moving through a series of manageable steps that are much more within your line of sight and immediate control. You may even find that once you get to that next step in your trajectory and learn from it, you will decide to move in what was a previously unthought-of direction.

By now you should be feeling more confident in your ability to reach your trajectory and feel excited about what lies ahead for you. Change and adaptation will be two of the most powerful weapons in your arsenal. Many experts in the field of human resources rate these two attributes as among the most important factors that will drive success in 2020. Raw technical skills are important, but can get dated quickly. It is for this reason that change and adaptation are so important to keep you current and relevant in your area. Be a constant learner and always seek opportunities to learn and expand your skills.

Many of you will recall the classic board game called the Game of Life. In it you must traverse various stages of life, with the goal of retiring with the most achievements and cash. You begin the game by placing your game piece in a position to "start your career" on the board. As you progress through the game you must select from a variety of choices related to your life and career. Along the way you encounter different obstacles, which could involve getting fired, experiencing a midlife crisis, or other challenges. Of course, this is just a game—but the lessons apply. The goal is to overcome obstacles and setbacks that occur and still win. The Game of Life is in many ways comparable to what you will do with your trajectory. The latter will just be on a grander scale and have more consequence.

   If you take away one thing from this book, it is to remember that you own your trajectory. The best thing you can do to prepare for your future—your trajectory—is to shape and influence it yourself. Everything we have discussed in this book is under your control. There are many books that will tell you how to get a job in a tough economy, how to bounce back after getting fired, and so on. However, those books all address something that has already occurred. By applying each of the seven lessons in this book you will set yourself up to avoid ever being in such a position in the first place. It can be said that those who fear losing their job the most, have the most to fear. They fear losing their job because they have not prepared for and adapted to change. They have not stayed current and avoided stagnation. Accordingly, these individuals will be among the first to be let go should there be an economic decline, organizational restructuring, or some other event that will result in the evaluation—and possible elimination—of some jobs. If you create a legacy of high and sustained performance, you will have less to fear.

Along your journey remember to pause for reflection and introspection. What have you accomplished recently? What have you not accomplished that you had expected to? Are your goals still the same now as last year? What have you learned? Are you living your life in accordance with your goals, priorities, and values? Doing this can be analogous to looking in the rearview mirror when driving. If you only look ahead you miss things behind you that are important. If you only look out the back window and focus on the past you will miss that which is important and right in front of you.

If you do not pause occasionally in order to consider what you are doing, you will impede your ability to stay on your trajectory. If you don't take time for reflection you may easily allow yourself to fall into a routine. When that happens you become a victim of your own habits, which you must not let constrain you. At the same time you should not spend too much time looking in that same rearview mirror. There is a reason that the windshield is bigger than the mirror: It is more important to focus on what is ahead of you than on what you left behind. You learn from the latter, occasionally look back to ensure that you don't repeat mistakes, and then look ahead.

I will leave you with this: Be true to yourself. Be true to others. This will be the authentic you. If you do, you will own your trajectory. Now go get it. Live your trajectory.

REFERENCES

INTRODUCTION

Society for Industrial and Organizational Psychology: www.
siop.org

GETTING STARTED: THE CONCEPT OF TRAJECTORY

Thomas Jefferson: http://www.monticello.org/site/jefferson/
brief-biography-thomas-jefferson; http://www.biography.
com/people/thomas-jefferson-9353715

Brendan Haas: http://abcnews.go.com/blogs/headlines/2012/
05/boy-who-donated-disney-trip-to-soldiers-family-wins-
vacation-of-his-own/

Ben Saunders: Speech at SuccessConnect, June 11, 2012
(San Francisco).

LESSON 1: THE POWER OF FEEDBACK

Harris, M. M., & Schaubroek, J. (2006). "A Meta-Analysis of Self-Supervisor, Self-Peer, and Peer-Supervisor Ratings." *Personnel Psychology* 41:43–62.

Coors Brewing translation error: http://www.clickz.com/clickz/column/2036234/marketing-translation-mistakes-learn

Schultz, H., & Gordon, J. (2011). *Onward: How Starbucks Fought for Its Life Without Losing Its Soul.* Emmaus, PA: Rodale.

Bazerman, M. H., & Chugh, D. (2006). "Decisions Without Blinders." *Harvard Business Review* 84.

Perman, S. (2010). *In-N-Out Burger: A Behind-the-Counter Look at the Fast-Food Chain That Breaks All the Rules.* New York: Collins Business.

Walton, S., & Huey, J. (1993). *Made in America.* New York: Bantam Books.

Bandura, A., Ross, D., & Ross, S. A. (1961). "Transmission of Aggression Through Imitation of Aggressive Models." *Journal of Abnormal and Social Psychology* 63:575–582.

LESSON 2: PERSISTENCE AS A DIFFERENTIATOR

Mandela, N. (1995). *Long Walk to Freedom: The Autobiography of Nelson Mandela.* Boston: Little, Brown & Company.

Ability × Persistence: Campbell, J. P., McColy, R. A., Oppler, S. H., & Sager, C. E. (1993). "A Theory of Performance."

In N. Schmitt & W. C. Borman, eds., *Personnel Selection in Organizations*, 35–70. San Francisco: Jossey-Bass.

Hawk, T. (2010). *How Did I Get Here?: The Ascent of an Unlikely CEO*. Hoboken, NJ: Wiley.

Yerkes, R. M., & Dodson, J. D. (1908). "The Relation of Strength of Stimulus to Rapidity of Habit-Formation." *Journal of Comparative Neurology and Psychology* 18: 459–482.

American Psychological Association study: http://www.apa.org/helpcenter/willpower.aspx

Pearson, K. (1903). "Mathematical Contributions to the Theory of Evolution: II. On the Influence of Natural Selection on the Variability and Correlation of Organs." *Royal Society Philosophical Transactions* 200:1–66.

Steven Kaplan CEO study: Kaplan, S. N., Klebanov, M. M., & Sorensen, M. (2012). "Which CEO Characteristics and Abilities Matter?" *Journal of Finance* 67:973–1007. http://www.bloomberg.com/news/2011-10-26/persistence-is-best-predictor-of-ceo-success-steven-n-kaplan.html

Tough, Paul (2012). *How Children Succeed: Grit, Curiosity, and the Hidden Power of Character*. Boston: Houghton Mifflin Harcourt.

Boston Market: http://www.entrepreneur.com/article/81172

Perman, S. (2010). *In-N-Out Burger: A Behind-the-Counter Look at the Fast-Food Chain That Breaks All the Rules*. New York: Collins Business.

Luttrell, M. (2009). *Lone Survivor: The Eyewitness Account of Operation Redwing and the Lost Heroes of SEAL Team 10*. Boston: Little, Brown & Company.

Aesop (1867). Aesop's Fables: The Hare and the Tortoise.

Under Armour Willpower watch: http://www.underarmour. com/shop/us/en/armour39

LESSON 3: THINK BIG, ACT SMALL, MOVE QUICK

Bob Gibson stats: http://www.baseball-reference.com/ players/g/gibsobo01.shtml

Ripken, C. Jr., & Bryan, M. (1997). *The Only Way I Know.* New York: Viking.

Smith, E. (2011). *Game On: Find Your Purpose—Pursue Your Dream.* Carol Stream, IL: Tyndale House Publishers.

Ben Saunders: Speech at SuccessConnect, June 11, 2012 (San Francisco).

Bass, D., Wells, F., & Ridgeway, R. (1998). *Seven Summits.* New York: Warner Books.

Locke, E. A., & Latham, G. P. (2002). "Building a Practically Useful Theory of Goal Setting and Task Motivation: A 35-Year Odyssey." *American Psychologist* 57:705–717.

Mischel, W., Yuichi, S., & Rodriguez, M. L. (1989). "Delay of Gratification in Children." *Science* 244:933–938.

Creswell, J. D., Bursley, J. K., & Satpute, A. B. (2013). "Neural Reactivation Links Unconscious Thought to Decision Making." *Social Cognitive and Affective Neuroscience* 8.

Wilson, T. D., & Schooler, J. W. (1991). "Thinking Too Much: Introspection Can Reduce the Quality of Preferences and Decisions." *Journal of Personality and Social Psychology* 60:181–192.

Grove, A. S. (1996). *Only the Paranoid Survive: How to Exploit the Crisis Points That Challenge Every Company*. New York: Currency Doubleday.

Napoleon: www.historyofwar.org

Sims, P. (2011). *Little Bets: How Breakthrough Ideas Emerge from Small Discoveries*. New York: Free Press.

LESSON 4: BREAKING THROUGH PLATEAUS

Gerstner, L. V. Jr. (2002). *Who Says Elephants Can't Dance? Inside IBM's Historic Turnaround*. New York: HarperBusiness.

Grove, A. S. (1996). *Only the Paranoid Survive: How to Exploit the Crisis Points That Challenge Every Company*. New York: Currency Doubleday.

Burke, M. (2012). *4th and Goal: One Man's Quest to Recapture His Dream*. New York: Business Plus.

Nola Ochs: http://goforthaysstate.com/s/947/index. aspx?pgid=1028

Csíkszentmihályi, M. (1990). *Flow: The Psychology of Optimal Experience*. New York: Harper & Row.

Ericsson, K. A., Krampe, R. Th., & Tesch-Romer, C. (1993). "The Role of Deliberate Practice in the Acquisition of Expert Performance."*Psychological Review* 100:363–406.

CNN: http://money.cnn.com/2012/06/29/technology/rim-blackberry-10/index.htm

Forbes: http://www.forbes.com/sites/larrymagid/2012/06/
29/happy-5th-birthday-iphone-you-changed-everything/

Lafley, A. G., & Charan. R. (2008). *The Game-Changer: How You Can Drive Revenue and Profit with Innovation.* New York: Crown Business.

Duncker, K. (1945). "On Problem-Solving." Translated by L. S. Lees. *Psychological Monographs* 58:i–113.

Kim, W. C., & Mauborgne, R. (2005). *Blue Ocean Strategy: How to Create Uncontested Market Space and Make Competition Irrelevant.* Boston: Harvard Business Review Press.

LESSON 5: AVOIDING THE STAGNATION TRAP

GE & DJIA: http://money.cnn.com/2009/06/01/news/
companies/dow_jones/

Beddoes, Z. M. (2011). "The Year of Self-Induced Stagnation." From *The Economist: The World in 2012* print edition.

Slywotzky, A. J., & Weber, K. (2011). *Demand: Creating What People Love Before They Know They Want It.* New York: Crown Business.

Christensen, C. (2003). *The Innovator's Dilemma: The Revolutionary Book That Will Change the Way You Do Business.* New York: Harper Collins.

Gladwell, M. (2000). *The Tipping Point: How Little Things Can Make a Big Difference.* Boston: Little, Brown & Company.

AIG: http://www.thenation.com/article/153929/aig-bailout-scandal?page=0,0

Mario Lemieux: http://www.nhl.com/ice/news.htm?id= 658116

Daniels, A. C. (2000). *Bringing Out the Best in People: How to Apply the Astonishing Power of Positive Reinforcement.* New York: McGraw-Hill.

Internet search market share: http://www.comscore.com/ Insights/Press_Releases/2013/1/comScore_Releases_ December_2012_U.S._Search_Engine_Rankings

LESSON 6: ACHIEVING GROWTH FROM FAILURE

Josephson, M. (1992). *Edison: A Biography.* New York: Wiley.

Seligman, M. E. P., & Maier, S. F. (1967). "Failure to Escape Traumatic Shock." *Journal of Experimental Psychology* 74:1–9.

Baumeister, R. F., Bratslavsky, E., Finkenauer, C., & Vohs, K. D. (2001). "Bad Is Stronger Than Good." *Review of General Psychology* 5:323–370.

Edmundson, A. C. (2011)."Strategies for Learning from Failure." *Harvard Business Review* 89:48–55.

Moore, L. K. (2011). *Funding Emergency Communications: Technology and Policy Considerations.* Congressional Research Service.

Amadeo Giannani: http://www.time.com/time/magazine/
article/0,9171,989772,00.html; http://www.entrepreneur.
com/article/197632

San Francisco earthquake: http://www.archives.gov/legislative/
features/sf/

John Grisham: http://www.jgrisham.com/bio/

Doolittle Raid: http://www.doolittleraider.com/

Harford, T. (2011). *Adapt: Why Success Always Starts with
Failure*. New York: Farrar, Straus and Giroux.

Mars Orbit: http://www.inspirationmars.org

Team Dimensions Profile 2.0 Research Report (2006). In-
scape Publishing, Inc.

Cascading Failure: http://eioc.pnnl.gov/research/
2003blackout.stm; http://www.scientificamerican.com/
article.cfm?id=2003-blackout-five-years-later

Bureau d'Enquêtes et d'Analyses pour la sécurité de
l'aviation civile—France (2002). Accident on 25 July
2000 at La Patted'Oie in Gonesse (95) to the Concorde
registered F-BTSC operated by Air France (Trans.).

J. C. Penney: http://www.nytimes.com/2013/04/10/business/
how-an-apple-star-lost-his-luster-at-penneys.
html?pagewanted=all&_r=0; http://finance.yahoo.com/
blogs/breakout/ron-johnson-jcpenney-anatomy-retail-
failure-114635276.html; http://business.time.com/2013/
04/09/the-5-big-mistakes-that-led-to-ron-johnsons-ouster-
at-jc-penney/; http://www.fastcompany.com/3008059/
ron-johnsons-5-key-mistakes-jc-penney-his-own-words

Amabile, T. M., & Kramer, S. J. (2011). *The Progress Principle: Using Small Wins to Ignite Joy, Engagement, and*

Creativity at Work. Boston: Harvard Business Press Books.

Goldberg, L. R. (1993). "The Structure of Phenotypic Personality Traits." *American Psychologist* 48:26–34.

Minbashian, A., Earl, J., & Bright, J. E. H. (2013). "Openness to Experience as a Predictor of Job Performance Trajectories." *Applied Psychology: An International Review* 62:1–12.

LESSON 7: SUSTAINING OUTLIER PERFORMANCE

Smith, E. (2011). *Game On: Find Your Purpose—Pursue Your Dream*. Carol Stream, IL: Tyndale House Publishers.

Russian Olympics: Scaglione, R., & Cummins, W. (1993). *Karate of Okinawa: Building Warrior Spirit*. New York: Person-to-Person Publishing.

Michael Phelps visualization: http://www.washingtonpost.com/sports/olympics/michael-phelps-has-mastered-the-psychology-of-speed/2012/06/13/gJQAHiQuZV_story.html

Bandura, A. (1982). "Self-Efficacy Mechanism in Human Agency." *American Psychologist* 37:122–147.

Rosenthal, R., & Jacobson, L. (1968). *Pygmalion in the Classroom: Teacher Expectation and Pupils' Intellectual Development*. New York: Holt, Rinehart & Winston.

Madon, S., Guyll, M., Spoth, R., & Willard, J. (2004). "Synergistic Effect: Self-Fulfilling Prophecies: The Synergistic Accumulative Effect of Parents' Beliefs on

Children's Drinking Behavior." *Psychological Science* 15:837–845.

Achor, S. (2010). *The Happiness Advantage.* New York: Crown Business.

Mycoskie, B. (2011). *Start Something That Matters.* New York: Spiegel & Grau.

INDEX